Supporting the Journey of English Learners after Trauma

JUDITH B. O'LOUGHLIN &
BRENDA K. CUSTODIO

University of Michigan Press
Ann Arbor

Copyright © by the University of Michigan 2020
Published in the United States of America
The University of Michigan Press
Printed and bound by CPI Group (UK) Ltd, Croydon, CR0 4YY

ISBN-13: 978-0-472-03797-1 (print)
ISBN-13: 978-0-472-12912-6 (ebook)

2024   2023   2022   2021   4   3   2   1

We dedicate this book to the memory of
Joseph John O'Loughlin (1946–2020),
husband, father, and grandfather.
Joseph supported both authors in their
efforts from conception to
completion of this book. Although never
a teacher, he was an ardent advocate
for immigrant students.

Acknowledgments

Grateful acknowledgment is given to these individuals and publishers for permission to reprint their work or previously published materials.

Jenna Altherr-Flores for giving us permission to quote from her presentation at the 2018 TESOL Convention, Chicago. Used with permission.

Bernard van Leer Foundation (the Netherlands) for Dr. Edith Grotberg's "I Have, I Am, I Can" model. Copyright © 1995. Used with permission.

Collaborative for Academic, Social, and Emotional Learning (CASEL) for the adaptation of its self-assessment tool in the Checklist of SEL Competencies. Copyright © 2017. Used with permission.

Dr. John Harrison for the use of his table on the Salutogenic Effect. Copyright © 2007. Used with permission.

National Center on Safe Supportive Learning Environments (NCSSLE) for the use of the information found in their Secondary Traumatic Stress and Self-Care Packet to develop our Self-Care Survey. Used with permission.

Oxford Publishing Limited for adaptations to Summary Table of Risk and Protective Factors for Immigrant Children from *Supporting and Educating Traumatized Students*. Copyright © 2013. Used with permission.

Spring Institute for material from the grid on preventative mental health in *Cultural Adjustment, Mental Health, and ESL*. Copyright © 1999. Used with permission.

TESOL International for *The 6 Principles for Exemplary Teaching of English Learners®: Grades K–12*. Copyright © 2018 TESOL International Association. All rights reserved. Used with permission.

Every effort has been made to contact the copyright holders for permission to reprint borrowed material. We regret any oversights that may have occurred and will rectify them in future printings.

Contents

Introduction

One of the hottest topics in education today is trauma-informed pedagogy. Much of what has been written in this area comes from counselors, therapists, and other experts in this field. We are in no way claiming to be mental health professionals. However, we do know about English learners, and we have found very little written specifically about the effects of trauma on this specific population. It is our desire to sift through the literature on trauma and social-emotional learning and find the kernels that apply directly to English learners.

We know that not all English learners have experienced trauma, but unfortunately too many have been victims of events that could have produced traumatic memories—some as second language (L2) students who were born in the United States, some as immigrants before their arrival into the U.S., and others as immigrants after their arrival in the U.S. It is our desire to help educators better understand the possible traumatic backgrounds of our students and how it could be affecting their academic, social, and emotional lives now. But most important, we want our focus to be on how we can help to create a safe environment in our schools and in our classrooms that will help each child recognize, nurture, and expand their own internal resilience that has enabled them to weather their past situations and that will allow them to continue the healing process.

This book was written mainly for teachers of students with immigrant backgrounds and also for the building administrators who support them. Our audience will include mainstream teachers, bilingual and ESL/ELD teachers, as well as teachers of special populations. Other school support personnel such as counselors, paraprofessionals, and social workers will also benefit from learning about the impact of traumatic experiences on their L2 students. We certainly do not want to stigmatize or overgeneralize; we are not looking for pity, but for empathy. We want to inform and offer suggestions. We cannot help someone if we do not understand their situation. Our deepest desire is for all students to have their basic academic and emotional needs met in our classrooms. In order for this to happen, teachers must truly know their students and have the skills and tools to best meet those needs.

We begin with a foundational chapter focused on the types of trauma many immigrants and their families have faced and may still be facing. Then we moved to three ways schools and teachers can support these students. First, creating trauma-sensitive schools and classrooms provides the necessary atmosphere of safety and support. Second, we move to specific activities designed to help each learner recognize their own internal strengths and move toward a positive self-identity. Then we explore the critical nature of a team response to resilience. We work in waves from the student needs to the teacher needs, and then out to the broader environment, including school support personnel, the family, and the community. We end with a caution that only when educators practice self-care can they remain in a position to offer the maximum assistance to their students.

Our goal was to help our readers discover resources to move English learners from trauma to resilience within the school environment, focusing on social-emotional learning (SEL) practices in the classroom and beyond. Finally, we are certainly aware of and must warn readers that schools may at times need to seek outside resources and assistance from health care professionals who are trained to address trauma beyond the school setting.

It is our desire that this book will offer educators information on the types of issues many of our L2 learners have faced or may still be facing and to provide specific, practical activities that a teacher and a school can apply to enable students to recognize and build on their individual motivations and strengths that can support their journey from trauma to resilience.

Each chapter contains a section called For Further Study that is designed to provide the educator alone or in teams and/or study groups with the opportunity to go beyond the chapter's contents to explore topics in more depth. Individual teachers, teacher study groups, support staff, and administrators can choose to focus on one topic or on several topics and then share their expanded understandings of how it might be applied in an educational setting.

A Note on Terminology: There are several terms that we feel need to be introduced before you read this book. We are combining the complex and sensitive fields of immigration and trauma-informed teaching and both have their own vocabulary and history. We hope that this list of basic terminology will help lay the foundation for your journey by understanding how the terms are used in this book.

We also want to add that education does not exist in a bubble. What happens in the country and the world impacts both the students and their classrooms. Our immigration policy is extremely political and changes constantly. We have tried to focus on the role that immigration has on children, realizing that by the time you read this book, new policies may be in place with different implications for students.

- An **immigrant** is a person who was born outside the United States and who has moved to this country with the intention to live here indefinitely. We use it as an overarching term. Immigrants can include people who enter the United States through various legal channels such as family reunification or through the visa lottery program, as well as individuals (children and adults) who enter the United States without the proper documentation or who overstay their temporary visas.

- A **refugee** is a person with legal immigrant status granted outside the U.S. based on having experienced persecution. Refugees are permitted to apply for citizenship after a certain amount of time determined by the government. A refugee is one sub-category of an immigrant.

- An **asylee**, or **asylum-seeker,** is another category of immigrant. They are individuals who enter the United States and then ask for official permission to stay. They must prove a well-founded fear of persecution the same as a refugee, but the difference is that they ask after they enter the U.S., not before. The U.S. government does not consider asylees as refugees until and unless their case is approved. How this is handled and who is permitted to stay varies depending on the national political situation. The individuals and families who are arriving at the southern border and are asking for political asylum fall into this latter category. When we use the term *immigrant*, we are most often referring to all categories.

- A **newcomer** is a student who has been in the United States less than two years and who has developing English skills. Some of the activities listed in Chapter 3 will be specifically appropriate for these new arrivals. The term does not refer to the immigration status of the student but to the length of time in the country.

- **SIFE/SLIFE** both refer to students who have experienced an interruption in their education. **SIFE** is the older of the two acronyms and stands for Students with Interrupted Formal Education. The newer term growing in popularity is **SLIFE** (Students with Limited or Interrupted Formal Education), with the *L* added to refer to the fact that some of these students have more than just interrupted schooling—it may be limited or, in some cases, non-existent. Students with interrupted educations face a number of challenges in U.S. schools. While not all SLIFE have experienced situations that may have resulted in trauma, many come from areas of the world where violence is common and may be the impetus for their relocation. Also, for many of these students, the stress of trying to make up for their lost years of education can create its own type of trauma.

- **Resilience** is defined in this book as the ability to adapt in the face of adversity and trauma to those stressors that may have impacted the learner's ability to survive and thrive. We do not look at it as "bouncing back" from a difficult or a perceived challenging experience. For the learners described in this book, becoming resilient is empowering and allows the individual to grow and significantly improve his/her life. We understand that the term *resilience* has received some negative reaction because in certain situations it has been used it to place the blame on the victim, arguing that if the person with the challenge had just been stronger, if they had more resilient, then the situation would have been easily resolved. This is absolutely not how we are using this term. We recognize that the situations our students have faced were out of their control, and we are offering support to help them channel their own inner strengths to rebuild their lives and move beyond their earlier circumstances. We are trying to provide a helping hand within an atmosphere of safety and empathy.

Terms that are defined in the Glossary appear in boldface on first mention in this book.

1

The Trauma of English Learners: Beginning the Journey to Resilience

---

The addressing of trauma within school settings is not only feasible but also fully consistent with and supportive of the primary goals of academic programs. A trauma-sensitive environment is one that is, to the degree possible, safe and attuned to the needs of students, families, staff, and the community. Such an environment supports the academic competence of all students, whether trauma impacted or not; provides tools to support students and staff with managing emotional and behavioral challenges; supports teachers and other staff in negotiating difficult situations, often reducing stress and burnout among teaching staff; and ultimately, has the potential to increase positive outcomes among youth across domains.
—Blaustein, 2013, p. 13

We believe the best way to help all children is to develop a strong enough relationship with each student so that we, as educators, are able to notice small but significant changes that may signal internal struggles. We wrote this book to explore the **trauma** faced by various immigrant populations, both before departure and after arrival in their new communities. Other second language (**L2**) learners who may have been born in the United States have concerns about the immigration status of family members, live in a toxic anti-immigrant atmosphere, or reside in neighborhoods rife with poverty and violence that pervade their daily lives and result in what many researchers call **chronic stress**. Trauma for the L2 student can manifest itself visibly with overt signs or invisibly as an internalized fear.

What can be done to provide a welcoming, non-threatening environment in the school and assist students on their journey to becoming resilient learners? What is the role of the classroom teacher and other educational professionals on this journey? Is it even realistic to expect a teacher to provide assistance in an area for which very few educators have any formal training? And how can we do this without falling victim to the very stress and trauma we are working to ameliorate?

What Is Trauma? What Are the Long-Term Effects of Trauma on Youth?

Several definitions of trauma exist, but most are based on the concept that some experience, or group of experiences, has occurred that caused fear, and this experience is overwhelming and contained some level of threat toward the individual or someone close to them. The threat could be physical, mental, emotional, or a combination of all three. According to Blaustein (2013), "These exposures may be acute or chronic. An **acute stressor** is one that is typically sudden and of a relatively brief duration. **Chronic stressors** are those that occur over time and involve layers of experience or repeated exposures" (p. 5). It is this chronic stress that is often the most dangerous and unfortunately all too common for many L2 learners, both those born in the U.S. and those who came as immigrants or refugees. Chronic stress is also known as **complex trauma** and it may result in more problematic challenges because it affects a student's ability to complete daily tasks inside and outside the classroom.

This book focuses on the cumulative or chronic trauma often associated with migration. While this type of trauma may be more difficult to diagnose because of the multiple causes, it is critical that educators address the symptoms when possible and find ways to help students learn to deal with their situation and move forward. As classroom teachers, without formal training in dealing with the adverse effects of trauma, what can we do? In most cases, it is not our responsibility as educators to diagnose or treat in a clinical manner the results of this cumulative stress, but we are expected, as caring individuals, to create an atmosphere of safety and support that will allow students to reset their emotional equilibriums and then build on that secure foundation. To best do this, we need to understand to some degree what the student has experienced and what types of situations might **trigger** emotional responses. We need to realize that some academic or behavioral actions may be grounded in past experiences and then need to take that into consideration when reacting. In extreme cases, we may need to refer the student for help beyond the classroom (see page 23).

How does exposure to long-term or complex trauma affect children? Susan Craig (2017), in her book about trauma and adolescents, says that "early trauma limits adolescents' ability to use higher-order thinking to regulate subcortical brain activity. Their thinking is 'held hostage' by relentless fear and hyperarousal that derail focus needed to achieve academically. Frustrated, teens with trauma histories often disengage from school" (p. 7). For English learners, this can affect their ability to focus on language development, concentrate on extensive reading passages, create and edit written assignments, or sit for extended periods of time. All of these activities are critical for academic success, especially at the secondary level. In addition to academic problems, chronic stress can lead to issues in other areas as well.

Another leader in the field of traumatic stress in children, Joel Ristuccia (2013), states that trauma places children "at significant risk for a host of social, emotional, academic, and cognitive impairments, and these impairments may create barriers to learning that lead to difficulties in school, risk-taking behaviors and long-term social, occupational, and health issues" (p. 253).

Some of the common manifestations of trauma in school-age children are listed. The list comes from the Child Trauma Toolkit for Educators (The National Child Traumatic Stress Network, 2008, p. 10):

- anxiety, fear, and worry about safety of self and others (especially family members)

- worry about recurrence of violence

- changes in behavior such as an increase in activity level, decreased attention and/or concentration, withdrawal from others or activities, angry outbursts and/or aggression, and/or absenteeism

- increased somatic complaints (e.g., headaches, stomachaches)

- changes in school/academic performance

- over- or under-reacting to noise, physical contact, or sudden movements

- statements and questions about death and dying

■ difficulty with authority, redirection, or criticism

■ re-experiencing the trauma (e.g., nightmares or disturbing memories)

■ **hyperarousal** (e.g., sleep disturbance, tendency to be easily startled)

■ avoidance behaviors (e.g., resisting going to places that remind them of the event)

■ emotional numbing (e.g., seeming to have no feeling about the event)

At the elementary level, these manifestations may appear with students being clingier than usual with the teacher or parent while showing increased levels of distress (being unusually whiny, irritable, or moody). They will often exhibit a distrust of others, affecting how they interact with both adults and peers. Sometimes it may even result in the student recreating the event by repeatedly talking about, "playing" out, or drawing the event, although this is less common.

At the secondary level, students may act irritably with friends, teachers, or at events (more than the usual teen angst!). They may show discomfort with their feelings (such as troubling thoughts of revenge) and not realize how to express these uncomfortable feelings. Quite often there will be an increase in impulsivity or risk-taking behavior such as substance abuse or rule-breaking. They will demonstrate negative trust in friends or family that they had shown closeness to in the past. And, finally and probably the most frightening, there may be repetitive thoughts and comments about death or dying (including suicidal thoughts; writing, art, or notebook covers about violent or morbid topics; and internet searches on these topics). **Always take these signs seriously and seek professional help if this type of behavior surfaces.**

This list is not exhaustive, but it includes the most common symptoms of a student internally dealing with trauma. We also need to be aware that some students who have experienced multiple stressful events may rarely or never express any symptoms. It's worth noting that it is sometimes the students who do not show any overt symptoms that we need to watch more closely because they may be internalizing their fear and frustration and what appears to be unrelated actions may actually be a cry for help: "They may have symptoms of avoidance and depression that are just as serious as those of the acting out student. Try your best to take the child's traumatic experiences into consideration when dealing with acting out behaviors" (The National Child Traumatic Stress Network, 2008, p. 9).

What Causes Trauma in Immigrant and Refugee Youth?

While many of the issues immigrant and refugee children face may be similar, others may be specific to their situations. Many of these issues may be personal in nature while others are predominately focused on academics. DeCapua, Smathers, and Tang (2009, p. 40) list these non-academic or affective needs as those that can influence a student's ability to adjust and succeed:

- social, emotional, and psychological isolation due to family separation
- difficulty developing formation of social identity
- unclear sense of belonging and purpose
- limited community support network
- cultural adjustment difficulty

We will look at three specific groups of immigrant-background students who are most often affected by early traumatic experiences. The first group are youth who come as refugees, either with their family or alone, as **unaccompanied refugee minors**. The other two immigrant groups are recent arrivals from Latin America and children living in mixed status households. While there are certainly other immigrants who have difficult experiences, the overwhelming majority of our trauma-background students come from one of these three categories.

Trauma Faced by Refugee Youth

Refugees, probably more than any other immigrant group, have undoubtedly experienced complex trauma. They have been forced to leave most if not all of their previous life behind in their fight for survival. Jobs, homes, schools, possessions, friends, and often extended family members are abandoned, without knowledge of what lies ahead. David Starr, an elementary school principal in western Canada, interviewed several of the parents of his students and wrote their stories in a book titled *From Bombs to Books*. In it, one mother describes her refugee experience this way: "This is my story of being in a war, of being a refugee. It's a terrible thing, so terrible for everyone but especially for the children and the women. I was a little girl when the war started and a woman when I finally found safety. In those in-between years, I lost my youth and my innocence. Sometimes I still cry, you know? Sometimes I feel guilty that I'm alive, that maybe I shouldn't be here and that it isn't fair I survived while so many others didn't. But then I remember that the Lord saved me so that my child could live" (Starr, 2011, p. 98).

RoseMarie Perez Foster (2001), a leader in the field of trauma in immigrant youth, looks at trauma as a result of the series of events that covers from the initial situation in the home country that causes the flight to adjustment after resettlement in a third country; she uses the term **perimigration** to cover all events pre-, mid- and post-migration. The National Child Traumatic Stress Network's 2007 *Culture and Trauma Brief* described perimigration trauma as psychological distress that can occur during four parts of the migration process:

1. *events before migration,* such as extreme poverty, war exposure, and/or torture

2. *events during migration,* such as parental separation, hunger, and/or death of traveling companions

3. *the difficulty of continued rejection and suffering while seeking asylum,* such as chronic deprivation of basic needs

4. *survival as an immigrant,* including substandard living conditions, lack of sufficient income, and racism

It is obvious, therefore, that refugees will certainly fall into the category of those who have experienced chronic traumatic events. While some younger children may not have experienced or remember the pre-flight drama, they might either remember life in a refugee camp or they may have heard their parents talk about the difficulties of such a time. They will recognize that life in their new land came at a price and may wonder why their parents feel torn between the "home country" and their new life. Older youth and teens will feel this dichotomy even stronger and face new stressors as they move through adolescence, living between two worlds. Some of the situations common among refugee children that may have led to stress or trauma are listed on the National Child Traumatic Stress Network website:

1. *Traumatic stress* occurs when a child experiences an intense event that threatens or causes harm to his or her emotional and physical well-being. Refugees can experience traumatic stress related to:
   - war and persecution
   - displacement from their home
   - flight and migration
   - poverty
   - family/community violence

2. *Resettlement stress* involves stressors that refugee children and families experience as they try to make a new life for themselves, such as:
   - financial stressors
   - difficulties finding adequate housing
   - difficulties finding employment
   - loss of community support
   - lack of access to resources
   - transportation difficulties

3. *Acculturation stress* comes from stressors that refugee children and families experience as they try to navigate between their new culture and their culture of origin, such as:
   - conflicts between children and parents over new and old cultural values
   - conflicts with peers related to cultural misunderstandings
   - the need to translate for family members who are not fluent in English
   - problems trying to fit in at school
   - struggles to form an integrated identity, including elements of their new culture and their culture of origin

4. *Isolation stress* is a result of stressors that refugee children and families may experience as minorities in a new country, such as:

- feelings of loneliness and loss of social support network
- discrimination
- experiences of harassment from peers, adults, or law enforcement
- experiences with others who do not trust the refugee child and family
- feelings of not fitting in with others
- loss of social status

For children and adolescents, with the majority of their day spent at school, so much of their self-esteem comes from their ability to be academically and socially accepted. In addition to the stress experienced as a result of the refugee resettlement itself comes the frustration of trying to fit in, to look like and sound like their peers, and to be seen as competent students. For many refugee students who have limited or even no access to adequate education in the refugee camps, the ability to do well in school is hampered by gaps in their academic knowledge and skills in addition to their limited English proficiency. They are experiencing what Van der Veer (1998, p. 4) terms "**pedagogical neglect**." For more detailed information on the effects of interrupted education, see *Students with Interrupted Formal Education: Bridging Where They Are and What They Need* (Custodio & O'Loughlin, 2017).

According to Craig (2017), "By definition, trauma involves exposure to experiences that exceed one's capacity to cope. . . . It is, therefore, not difficult to imagine the incredible stress involved in being held to a level of performance and accountability that exceeds the developmental expectations of one's age. *This is especially true when the failure to live up to these unrealistic expectations is labeled as proof of a poor attitude and judged worthy of disciplinary action*" (p. 8, emphasis added). This feeling of inadequacy applies even more to refugees and other displaced immigrants who have not only lived through chronic traumatic experiences but are now placed in academic situations for which they are not prepared. As educators we must make sure that we are not punishing a student for academic or behavioral actions or reactions to situations out of his or her control. As Carey and Kim (2010) have said:

> While refugee youth confront adversity on many different levels, academic difficulties present one of the prevailing stumbling blocks with far-reaching implications. Similar to the familiar role that education plays abroad in mitigating the effects of war-related trauma, providing structure and stability, advancing social and cognitive development, contributing to psychological and social well-being, enabling youth to regain hope and dignity, and preparing youth for constructive adulthood, education is vital to the healing, healthy *acculturation,* and future success of refugee youth in the United States. . . . For immigrant youth in particular, who are spending more time in school than ever before in U.S. history, engagement with schooling—including relationships formed and the acquisition of academic, linguistic, and cultural knowledge—will generally bring about the most profound transformation in their lives. (pp. 193–194)

The National Association of School Psychologists (2015) provides advice for educators of refugees on their website. First, the organization emphasizes that we need to understand and recognize stressors. Refugee children and youth are often traumatized from premigration and resettlement experiences. They may have been exposed to violence and combat, home displacement, malnutrition, detention, and torture. Many have been forced to leave their country and cannot safely return home. Some may have come without their parents and without knowing of their health or safety. Psychological stress and traumatic experiences are often inflicted upon these children over months or even years, and many have experienced some kind of discrimination once they entered U.S. schools. Additionally, they often resettle in high-poverty and high-crime neighborhoods, increasing exposure to stressful conditions.

Second, they state that teachers need to understand the effect of trauma on school functioning. Extreme stress, adversity, and trauma can impede concentration, cognitive functioning, memory, and social relationships. Additionally, stress can contribute to both internalized symptoms—such as **hypervigilance**, anxiety, depression, grief, fear, anger, isolation—and externalized behaviors—such as startle responses, reactivity, aggression, and conduct problems. Given the often chronic and significant stress placed on refugee students, many are at increased risk for developing trauma and other mental health disorders, undermining their ability to function effectively in school. Further, given the environment of their previous schooling and the immigration to the United States, many have experienced significantly interrupted schooling; coupled with language gaps, many students arrive unprepared to participate in school with their same-age peers.

The oversight of refugees worldwide is under the purview of the United Nations High Commissioner for Refugees (UNHCR). Periodically the UNHCR does a review of the state of education in the camps under their control. A 2019 document reported that 63 percent of primary age children in the camps were attending school compared to 91 percent worldwide and 24 percent of secondary age students in the camps were enrolled in school compared to 84 percent; it also reported that only 3 percent of young people in the camps had the opportunity to extend their education to the university level. This is one of the reasons that when children are finally resettled, such a large percentage are not prepared for grade-level education in their new country (UNHCR, 2019).

The Washington State Office of the Superintendent of Public Instruction compiled a document titled *The Heart of Learning and Teaching: Compassion, Resilience, and Academic Success* (Wolpow et al., 2009) to help their teachers understand and support children of trauma. While not specific to the refugee situation, the document listed five adverse effects of trauma on schooling:

1. Students who are victims of trauma are two and one-half times more likely to fail a grade.

2. Students who are victims of trauma score lower on standardized achievement tests.

3. Students who are victims of trauma have more receptive and expressive language difficulties (a definite problem for students just learning a new language).

4. Students who are victims of trauma are suspended or expelled more often.

5. Students who are victims of trauma are designated to special education more often.

This information makes it clear that children who have been victims of trauma, including refugees, need special supports in the school setting to help them with their language and literacy development, socialization skills, and general academic support. Much of this initial support is provided in the ESL or bilingual classroom as part of the orientation process, such as explaining how the school day will operate, social skills like turn-taking and lining up for activities, cafeteria and gym class etiquette, etc. At times educators may need to offer additional scaffolding such as **calming centers** (areas where students can sit and do something non-academic such as coloring, puzzles, or listening to music to help soothe and de-escalate); attention to routines at lunch, recess, or math time to provide structure; and specific academic supports to prevent academic distress. Some examples of academic support are providing home language dictionaries for class use, providing a buddy for new arrivals, having a designated time for each student to meet individually with the teacher each week, and offering one homework free pass each month. More specific classroom strategies will be provided in Chapter 3.

In addition to the symptoms listed on pages 7–8, refugee students may also demonstrate their internal fear by exhibiting what psychologists commonly refer to as "flight, fight, or freeze." These three reactions to stress may have a unique look in the classroom, as shown in Table 1.1.

Other ways in which students may react in school directly relates to their earlier trauma experiences. According to Craig (2017), "Teens with trauma histories use a trial-and-error approach to learning as opposed to one that involves planning and self-reflection. They are youth who 'act and then think' and give up easily in the face of new or challenging tasks. They

TABLE **1.1**

How Students May React to Stress in the Classroom

Flight	Fight	Freeze
• withdrawing • fleeing the classroom • skipping class • daydreaming • seeming to sleep • avoiding others • hiding or wandering • becoming disengaged	• acting out • behaving aggressively • acting silly • exhibiting defiance • being hyperactive • arguing • screaming/yelling	• exhibiting numbness • refusing to answer • refusing to get needs met • giving a blank look • feeling unable to move or act

Source: Souers, 2016, p. 29.

live in the moment and find it difficult to project a future where they can control what happens to them" (p. 77). It will be the role of the teacher to help them organize their schoolwork and to help them set short- and long-term goals. The teacher can serve in the role of cheerleader, monitor, and guide. This is a critical need because, all too often, parents of refugees are facing daunting issues in their own lives and are unfamiliar with the expectations of a Western school system, so it is the teachers who must step in and provide the type of support that parents typically play for non-refugee students.

In addition to academic difficulties faced by trauma survivors, emotions also affect the ability to be successful in a school setting. According to Schmelzer (2018), "When trauma is repeated, as it is in child abuse, domestic violence, community violence, or war, we don't wait to get caught off-guard. Instead, we unconsciously, yet wisely, build a system of defenses against being overwhelmed and getting caught off-guard again, because building defenses to withstand repeated trauma conserves our energy for survival. Instead of getting flooded with emotion—with terror, fear, and all the responses to it—we build walls, moats, and methods of escape. We go numb, we feel nothing, and we do whatever we have to in order to maintain our distance from ourselves and others" (p. 13). Therefore, again, it will be teachers who provide that safe and protective environment that enables the refugee student to eventually lower his or her defenses and allow normal emotions to surface. The role of the teacher in the life of a refugee child cannot be overstated. In some cases, they may be the lifeline that enables the child to move beyond their pain and fear and build a trauma-free future.

Trauma Faced by Recent Arrivals from Latin America

The second group of immigrant students most likely to have experienced traumatic situations are students who are coming from various areas in Latin America. Political and economic issues and natural disasters have pushed people from their homes in search of peace and security. The proximity to the United States and the historic pattern of economic and social refuge here draws thousands each year.

A large percentage of these Latino immigrants each year are children who come into the country undocumented, sometimes without an adult family member and many with the intent to be reunited with someone who came to the United States before them. The greatest percentage of these children, usually known by the label of **unaccompanied minor**, have come in the last decade from the three northern countries of Central America: Guatemala, El Salvador, and Honduras. This area, often referred to as the **Northern Triangle**, is rife with drug and gang violence.

According to Digby (2019), "For unaccompanied minors from Central America, the journey through to the U.S. is an irrefutable landmine of traumatic experiences" (p. 20). Almost half of these children report leaving their home country because of experiences of violence (including gang violence, violence perpetrated by organized crime or government, and/or sexual violence), about one-quarter report abuse at home, and many report they are hoping to reunite with parents or other family members living in the U.S. (Kennedy, 2014; Schwartz, 2018; UNHCR, 2014). In addition to the problems that forced these children to flee their homeland, they undertake an extremely dangerous journey alone or with other minors. And, finally, upon arrival they are at substantial risk of further victimization if they are taken into custody and then face an uncertain future that could include deportation back to the very situation from which they fled. Consequently, these children are experiencing higher rates of anxiety, behavior issues, and **post-traumatic stress disorder (PTSD)** than their immigrant counterparts (Alvarez & Alegria, 2016).

In the midst of the pull of independence and the push of colliding cultures, unaccompanied minors face: identity concerns; challenging socioeconomic and environmental conditions; vulnerability to trauma, stress, substance abuse disorders, depression, and other psychiatric disorders; and multiple barriers to obtaining needed treatment.

As stated, once unaccompanied minors arrive in the U.S., their trauma continues. Many of these children were left behind in the home country with a family member while a parent or older sibling made the dangerous journey north to find work and send money back for their care. When the children are finally reunited with family members, the work of putting the family back together is often rocky. Parents want to reestablish their authority with teens who have been relatively independent for years. Sometimes the parent has a new partner and maybe additional children, so occasionally children even find they are not welcome in the new family. Even in the best of relationships, the extensive separation takes time to overcome (Digby, 2019).

The children who are met at the border by federal agents are taken into custody for varying lengths of time until a family member is found. Because the children come without prior authorization, they must request political asylum to be able to stay even temporarily in the U.S. This request winds its way through the legal channels and, as of 2019, the percentage of child migrants denied asylum was 71 percent (Cheatham, 2020). If the request is eventually denied, the child is required to leave the U.S. The legal battle is draining on the child and the family, both financially and emotionally. The fear of deportation looms like a black cloud over both the child and the family. And for those children who were able to enter the U.S. without apprehension, they live in constant fear of exposure and capture. (See pages 19–21 for some of the emotional consequences of trying to live "under the radar.")

[*Note:* Recent data on asylum-seekers is difficult to obtain because of a number of changes since 2018 in immigration policy, known collectively as the Migration Protection Protocols. One of these changes is the "Stay in Mexico" policy, which drastically cut the ability for Mexicans to seek asylum and to obtain legal representation at the southern border. It requires asylum-seekers to remain in Mexico until their case is ready to be heard. For others, new policies have resulted in the automatic removal back to the home country of many asylum-seekers, even children. A related decision, the Safe Third Country policy, requires asylum-seekers to either apply in the first country they enter after leaving their home country or risk being sent back home to apply (American Immigration Council, 2020).]

An additional cause of trauma for many of these students is school itself. Many had limited or inadequate educations in their home country, and almost all did not attend school during the journey north (Digby, 2019; Lukes, 2015). Those apprehended at the border may have "attended" school in the detention centers, but this type of situation is certainly not conducive to academic concentration and success. If unaccompanied minors do ultimately make it to school, their age usually does not align with their grade level (that is, they may be 10 years old but not prepared for the typical work expected in a 4th grade classroom); this population of students are often referred to as SLIFE or SIFE. Of course, they are underprepared for the rigors of their new educational setting: "Even schools designed for immigrants and refugees can sometimes find themselves alarmingly unprepared to handle the gamut of academic needs represented by Latino SIFE, including recognizing these when they arrive in U.S. classrooms" (Digby, 2019, p. 22). For more about SIFE/SLIFE, see the Introduction.

The Traumatic Impact of Living Undocumented

The third large group of children who are often experiencing toxic levels of stress are those who live in homes with undocumented family members, sometimes referred to as **mixed status households**. While the majority of these children are Latinos, there are children from many parts of the world living in this situation. It is estimated by the Brookings Institution that there were about 10.5 million undocumented individuals in the United States in 2019 (Kamarck & Stenglein, 2019). People from Mexico constitute about half of this total (5.5 million); Central Americans comprise another 1.9 million; Asians from China, India, South Korea, and the Philippines total another 1 million; and the other 2 million are from almost every other country.

As of 2019, there were about 5.9 million children living in mixed status homes (with undocumented family members); some of these children are part of the 10.5 million mentioned who arrived as immigrants. But 75 percent of these children were born here and are actually U.S. citizens themselves (Interdisciplinary Association for Population Health Science, 2019). Regardless of the child's citizenship status, because one or both parents are living in fear of deportation, the child remains in a constant state of uncertainty and anxiety: "When I come home from school, will my parents be gone? Who will take care of me? Will I have to stay by myself? Will I have to leave?" Often the parents do not want to talk about this uncertain future with young children as a way to protect them from fear. Nevertheless, children can sense there is a problem or that something is wrong; they can feel that parents are trying to shield them from something. The unknown can be just as bad for them, if not worse, than the reality: "Children in mixed-status families frequently worry about family separation and can exhibit high levels of stress. Children whose parents have been deported or detained are more likely to experience a host of social concerns and mental health problems, including decreased school performance, depression and other internalizing problems such as anxiety, and externalizing problems such as aggression and conduct issues" (Interdisciplinary Association for Population Health Science, 2019, p. 2).

This uncertainty and anxiety follow the children to school. In one study of school personnel in 12 states that included 3,500 responses from 730 schools (Johnson, 2018), *fear* and *separation* were the two most common words used when describing students' immigration concerns. Thousands of educators, almost three-quarters of those surveyed, described how their students from immigrant families—the vast majority of whom are U.S.-born—were terrified that families and friends—and sometimes even that they themselves—would be picked up by immigration authorities. The teachers said that this anxiety made it difficult for students to learn and teachers to teach. Educators reported student absences, a decline in academic performance, and less involvement from parents as some of the impacts on immigrant students. In addition, this study (Johnson, 2018) found that:

- 84 percent of educators reported having immigrant students express concerns about immigration enforcement while at school, such as fear of their parents being taken away.

- nearly 90 percent of school administrators observed immigrant students experiencing behavioral or emotional problems, most often related to fear and anxiety.

To drive this point home and end this section on a positive note, one teacher shared this story with one of the authors of how trauma had affected a child in her class:

> When I first met this fourth-grade Latino boy, he had severe behavior issues. He was cussing, throwing objects in the classroom, and breaking things. As I was able to build a bond with the student, he gradually opened up to me and began sharing what was bothering him. He told me about how his father had walked across the desert to the get to the U.S., and that now his mother was scheduled to go to immigration court. He was so afraid that she would be deported, and he didn't know what would happen to him or to his family. I was able to get the boy into counseling with a local agency who came to the school and worked with him on a regular basis. The counselors were bilingual and had ties with the community. By the end of the year, things were going better with the student, both academically and emotionally.

So, what can you as a teacher do to help these vulnerable children? One researcher (Thorp, 2018, p. 36) says that "it is critical that teachers understand how the threat of parental detention and deportation affects children's social-emotional development, their behavior, and their academic performance. These children have unique needs directly related to their family's mixed immigration status. With this understanding, teachers can adopt strategies to support children who are living in fear." She also believes that it is essential that "teachers can communicate to these vulnerable children that their classrooms are safe spaces where they have allies and can safely voice their fears. Teachers can become skilled at addressing the behavioral and performance challenges that may arise when a child is experiencing separation or is living in an environment of heightened fear" (Thorp, 2018, p. 36).

While teachers are not immigration experts and can seldom provide any assistance in this arena, they can certainly provide a safe place for students over several hours in their day. Teachers also need to build the type of relationship with children so that when they need someone to talk to about their situation, they feel safe and comfortable enough to be able to share their fears and uncertainty with someone at the school. Some students will never open up to anyone outside the family and they may have been warned about doing so, but for the student who needs someone who cares and will listen, it may be school personnel to which they turn.

What Are the Challenges of Supporting All Students with Chronic Trauma?

The discussion so far has focused on the causes of chronic stress for refugee, immigrant, and mixed status children, and how this stress can impact children. It is obvious from the information that has been presented so far that academic and emotional support for traumatized students is critical. For most educators, the difficulty lies not in *whether* to provide support, but in *how* it can best be provided. We hope to offer practical suggestions in later chapters that can be delivered in the classroom and as part of the typical curriculum where/when possible. Chapter 2 will focus on classroom atmosphere and routines, while Chapter 3 will offer activities that will encourage students to acknowledge the abilities that they already possess that have enabled them to survive their past situations and move forward. There are, however, challenges to addressing chronic trauma and those will be discussed first.

One of the challenges involves how trauma is viewed by different cultures. According to Morland et al. (2013), matters are complicated "by the fact that mental health treatment is often associated with severe stigma in many cultures. Combined with the different interpretations of mental health, these symptoms based on cultural frames of reference result in immigrant families very rarely seeking mental health treatment for their children in the United States, even if it may be indicated. It is also likely that available treatments and interventions supporting trauma-affected students are not as effective for immigrant families due to language and cultural differences, creating additional barriers to children's education" (p. 57).

The stigma associated with mental health and the fear of being labeled "crazy" may mean that distress is kept hidden because the condition labeled as "crazy" is often perceived as a fixed condition and may be ostracizing from community (Green & Kelley, 2016). One potential solution to this issue was proposed by the principal of an elementary school with a large refugee population, who recommends locating counseling services within the school to work with students with emotional and behavioral challenges. (Starr, 2011, pp. 72–73). Because many immigrant families trust the school more than outside agencies, having support personnel inside the school building can help bridge this distrust.

In terms of other challenges when dealing with trauma in a school setting, Blaustein (2013, pp. 9–13) has identified these four areas of concern for educators:

1. Teachers sometimes see social and emotional issues as secondary to academics, either in importance to the child or to their particular classroom focus.

2. Teachers are overwhelmed at the prospect of, or feel unqualified to, identify traumatized youth.

3. Trauma may manifest itself in so many ways and at different times in a child's life that it is often difficult to assess and treat.

4. There is a lack of resources, including training for classroom teachers and other school personnel, as well as enough counselors and social workers to provide support.

While it is certainly true that teachers are not trained to identify and counsel students suffering from the aftermath of trauma, there are signs that, if observed by an educator, signify that it is time to refer the child for more intensive assistance. The typical actions and symptoms listed on pages 7–8 should be considered signs that there may be internal issues that the student is dealing with. If the symptoms persist, or especially if they intensify, it is definitely a time to ask for intervention.

DeCapua, Marshall, and Tang (2020, p. 26) provide this list of warning signs that indicate to teachers that students are experiencing serious problems:

- depression

- extreme tiredness or fatigue

- self-destructive behaviors

- illnesses related to stress such as stomachaches or headaches

- unusual anger or frustration

- significant increase or decrease in appetite

- withdrawal from group activities

They recommend that teachers first talk to students about possible causes and then "if appropriate, refer them to counseling/guidance services." The process for referral will vary within school districts and should be discussed with administration.

Adverse Childhood Experiences (ACEs)

Much of the discussion on children and trauma is based on a study begun in 1995 by Kaiser Permanente and the Centers for Disease Control and Prevention. This longitudinal study was created to look at the long-term effects of what they termed **adverse childhood experiences (ACEs)** on a person's health (Felitti et al., 1998). What the researchers found was that there is a strong link between early childhood trauma and later chronic disease and various social problems. It was also concluded that people who experience more than one traumatic event have a stronger likelihood of experiencing the resultant negative symptoms. A ten-question screening questionnaire corresponds to the ten areas of concern addressed in the study:

There are ten types of childhood trauma measured in the ACE Study. Five are personal-physical abuse, verbal abuse, sexual abuse, physical neglect, and emotional neglect. Five are related to other family members: a parent who is an alcoholic, a mother who is a victim of domestic violence, a family member in jail, a family member diagnosed with mental illness, and the disappearance of a parent through divorce, death or abandonment. (Felitti et al., 1998; acestoohigh.com)

One concern of using the ACEs questionnaire and research with English learners is that many of the issues that are the foundation of this study "may not capture the adverse experiences specific to immigrant families; in fact, it is possible that adverse experiences and environments that are specific to the immigrant experience are not reflected in traditional measures of ACE exposure" (Ramirez, 2017, p. 5). Some of the areas of trauma that are reflected in the ACEs questionnaire, which would only be used by a health professional, reflect difficulties also faced by native English–speaking children. For example, one study found that 46 percent of U.S.-born children have experienced at least one ACE, yet for Latino children the number is 76 percent. Also, 28 percent of Latino children have experienced four or more of these issues. For both the native and immigrant groups, parental divorce and economic hardship were the most prevalent ACE exposures (Ramirez, 2017). However, according to the Hispanic Community Health Study/Study of Latinos, many of the types of issues faced by recently arrived Latinos are not addressed by the ten areas covered in the ACEs study. As a result, a revised version of the ACEs that more accurately reflects the immigrant experience is provided in Figure 1.1. It shows the type of feel-

FIGURE **1.1**

ACEs for Immigrant and Second Language Students

1. I have seen family members in dangerous situations.
2. I had to leave my home and escape to a different country due to violence or fear.
3. I have seen or experienced some form of sexual assault on either a family member or myself.
4. At some time in my life, I was separated from immediate family members for more than a week.
5. At some time in my life, I did not have enough food to eat or a safe place to live.
6. At some time in my life, I was not able to have the health care I needed.
7. At some time in my life, I was unable to attend school for at least three months.
8. Someone in my family has abused alcohol or drugs.
9. I am sometimes afraid to go out of my house.
10. I have been laughed at or bullied because of my clothes, accent, or ethnic heritage.
11. Sometimes I feel like I don't really belong anywhere.
12. Sometimes I have to take on adult responsibilities for which I do not feel prepared.

Source: Questionnaire based on the ACEs of the World Health Organization and the CDC.

ings that could be used to reveal the trauma-inducing situations that too many immigrant children have faced, or are still facing, that may be contributing to their ability to adjust to their new life and move from trauma to **resilience**. This list is <u>not</u> intended to be used as a screening tool or to replace any screener that has been already tested and approved for use with children, but it is designed to represent the types of issues and difficulties faced by immigrants and children of immigrants. Through listening to the stories of their students and discussions with family members, educators may hear of similar situations that could have caused traumatic stress. This list can serve as a frame of reference to better understand the backgrounds of the students.

It is worth noting that the World Health Organization (WHO) is currently developing and field-testing an international version of the ACEs tool (known as ACE-IQ) that can be used in global settings and that may be more appropriate for immigrants. The WHO International Questionnaire contains a variation of the original ten topics but has 31 questions. At the time of writing of this book, it was not yet available for general use. Check the WHO website (who.int) for updates.

English Learners and the Resilience Process

Teachers need to feel empowered to support and encourage students' journeys to resilience. In 2016, the U.S. Department of Education released the Newcomer Tool Kit. In it, the Department acknowledged the value of focusing on the strengths of the students: "It is critical for educators to acknowledge newcomers' individual strengths, the resilience they developed through the immigration process, and their rich potential for building on life experiences and prior schooling" (U.S. Department of Education, 2016, p. 3). The Newcomer Tool Kit continues by adding that supporting students and building upon their inner strengths must begin with strong, caring relationships:

> While formal school programs are essential to meeting newcomers' social emotional needs, often it is the informal caring relationships between school staff and newcomers that matter most. Such relationships enable teachers to understand and tap into students' interests and attitudes to engage students and strengthen their learning experiences— and thereby bolster their academic success. (pp. 5–6)

While school and teachers are critical to the resilience process, they must work in conjunction with the other protective factors in the life of children. In a seminal study on refugee mental health, Van der Veer (1998) found three determinants of a person's ability to survive traumatic experiences:

1. Their own inner strengths observable from childhood, such as intelligence, social responsiveness, and quick recovery from illness.

2. Favorable family conditions, such as the presence of one reliable adult for assistance and care.

3. Conditions outside the home, such as a supportive school environment and strong community or religious ties, also called *social support*.

It is critical that educators acknowledge this three-pronged support system that many refugees, and we argue most immigrants, possess. It is also important that teachers assist students and their families to recognize and build upon this foundation, giving them the tools to move beyond the effects of their traumas. Morland and Birman (2020) describe this teamwork:

> Typical immigrant strengths include deep and broad family ties, an abiding faith in the value of education, and "immigrant optimism"—or the confidence that life will be better in the United States. In addition, many immigrants are motivated by strong religious beliefs and socio-centric values. These values prioritize family or community welfare over the individual's, keeping their lives focused on larger goals and helping them endure and adapt to ongoing and often quite dramatic changes in their lives.... There is growing evidence that protective factors and processes such as supportive relationships with teachers, peers, family, and the community can help mediate these risks, resulting in improved academic performance of even the most vulnerable immigrant children over time. (pp. 108–109)

For Further Study

Alone or with colleagues in your educational setting, consider one or all of these questions. How will your responses help to expand your knowledge and that of your peers about this population of learners?

1. Which of the three main categories of immigrants with traumatic backgrounds are in your classroom (refugees, newcomers, or children from mixed immigrant status households)? What symptoms of trauma have you observed with your students?

2. What types of experiences have you had helping students who are being reunited with family members after years of separation? How has your school been able to help these families through this transition?

3. What would you consider to be your biggest challenge in helping students with chronic stress?

4. After considering Figure 1.1, how can you use this list in your context? What would this information help you to provide or change?

2

Trauma-Sensitive Schools and Classrooms

Rather than turning a blind eye to the adversity in students' lives, staff members in trauma-sensitive schools are equipped to bear witness to its existence. In this non-stigmatizing environment, youth experience a sense of belonging and acceptance that is missing in other environments where they feel marginalized and alone. No longer needing to hide the stress in their lives, they are able to develop the skills they need to move beyond trauma and create a future for themselves. Validating students' life experiences in nonjudgmental ways is the cornerstone of a trauma-sensitive school.

—Craig, 2017, p. 14

A popular catch phrase across the country and around the world is the term **trauma-sensitive schools**. According to Craig, Massachusetts was the first state to coin this phrase, which it used to describe the "school climate, instructional designs, and policies needed to help traumatized students achieve academic and social competence" (2017, p. 10). But Craig also states that a school, or a teacher, does not actually have to mention the term *trauma* to be trauma-sensitive. It is not a label, but a mindset.

So, what does a trauma-sensitive school and classroom look like for an English learner? Are teachers and schools expected to do something different for an L2 learner who has experienced trauma than what they would do for a native English speaker? The answer is yes and no. The basic supports for a student who has experienced trauma will be similar regardless of language or culture. What may be different will be the challenge of finding supports that take into consideration the unique experiences, language, and cultural background of the L2 learner.

Teachers today are being asked to meet expectations that already seem unrealistic and insurmountable, and now they feel that they are being asked to also serve as quasi-counselors. Kristin Souers, in her 2017/2018 *Education Leadership* article on supporting students with trauma, says that "one of the biggest challenges of today's classrooms is being able to find a balance between the focus on academic growth and success and the provision of a safe and emotionally secure learning environment for all students" (p. 35). As you read this chapter, we hope that you will see that establishing a trauma-sensitive classroom is not changing or adding to the curriculum as much as following routines, showing sensitivity to the emotions and reactions of individual students, and being flexible when necessary. These are the same personality dispositions that are already expected of all teachers. This mindset is described in the ASCD's Whole Child tenets, developed to encourage a safe learning environment for all children: "Caring educators know that understanding and responding to what's causing distress at home is part of keeping each young person healthy, safe, engaged, supported and challenged" (Souers, 2017/2018, p. 33).

What Does a Trauma-Sensitive School and/or Classroom Look Like?

A trauma-sensitive school is only as effective as its teachers and staff and their interactions with the students. A number of common elements are found in most trauma-sensitive schools or classrooms, and while a teacher may not exhibit all of these characteristics, the list provided describes those that are the most common.

A trauma-sensitive teacher:

- sees students through a trauma-sensitive lens.
- creates opportunities for students to share issues in a safe environment and express and work through their feelings in a risk-free environment.
- is welcoming and open to all students.
- provides structure and routines without being inflexible.

- has a support system in place before a crisis occurs and plans for the unexpected.

- stays current on the political situations of the countries of the students in the classroom.

- has basic knowledge of the religious, social, and cultural backgrounds of each student.

- focuses on the social and emotional, as well as the academic, needs of the students.

Next, we show how each of these characteristics may appear in a school setting.

Seeing Students through a Trauma-Sensitive Lens

Looking at students through a trauma lens changes the fundamental question from What's wrong with this child? to What happened (or is happening) to this child? It looks at the meaning behind the behavior and changes the teacher's reaction from punishment to support and assistance (Bloom, 2014). A trauma lens would also change how we view the ability of the child to "do school." According to Birman, "The assumption is that it is the child who lacks the skills to handle the classroom, and not the classroom that needs to be changed in order to accommodate the needs of the child" (2002, p. 8).

Using the trauma-sensitive lens is important for both native English speakers and English learners because it puts the focus on the child, not the problem. Just as when we are taking pictures and the focus is on the object in the foreground, the background blurs and takes on secondary importance. This fundamental mindset shift is the key to trauma-informed teaching.

Creating a Safe and Risk-Free Environment

In her 2017 book about trauma and teens, Susan Craig says that "trauma-sensitive schools are safe zones which buffer students from external forces that threaten their potential, while at the same time fostering the skills teens need to regulate internal emotions and drives" (p. 5). She also believes that "the web of supportive relationships that characterize trauma-sensitive schools provides the safety that teens need to strengthen 'triggers' and work to prevent escalation of the fight, flight, or freeze phenomena." (See Table 1.1.) This type of environment is not specific to English learners but will definitely provide the type of atmosphere that is required for immigrant students with trauma backgrounds to feel safe and welcome. Specific examples of activities to help students build resilience and overcome their reaction to triggers are provided in Chapter 3.

Being Welcoming and Open to All Students

Every student knows if they are welcome into their new school within minutes of entering a building. From the signs in the hallway to the faces of the office staff, it is obvious if new (and possibly different) students are welcome or are seen as an inconvenience or worse. For L2 students, seeing evidence that their language and culture are recognized can be crucial in calming their nerves and setting a tone of acceptance. This issue is discussed in more detail in Chapter 5, which looks at what we call the **hidden curriculum**, or the impression a new arrival will have of the culture of a school when they first enter the building.

Providing Structure and Routines without Being Inflexible

Every article and book about children and trauma emphasizes the critical role that routines and structure play in their lives, and school is key here as a place where they feel the most comfortable and secure. Children know what to expect and what is expected of them in school, but they also need to practice independence and be able to make choices in an environment where those choices have less critical consequences. According to Wolpow et al. (2009), "The more powerless a child feels, the more likely trauma symptoms will return. Teacher-centered rules and consequences can trigger feelings of powerlessness. When triggered, children affected by trauma don't think. Instead they react.... [However], students struggling with the effects of trauma need structure and high expectations. They need to be empowered to succeed. They benefit from having real choices and control" (p. 71). Our role as educators is to find that balance between order and freedom, being in control and offering students a choice. It is often a fine line that requires flexibility on the part of the teacher.

Refugee trauma expert Dina Birman (2002) cautions that teachers need to carefully consider how best to provide structure and discipline within the framework of the classroom: "When children externalize symptoms of PTSD, service providers may feel reluctant to discipline the child or to insist that the child follow rules of behavior in school and other settings, fearing that this will further traumatize the child. However, when done in a caring way, setting limits and helping the child observe and monitor her own behavior is extremely helpful to the child, helps normalize the situation, and gives the child skills to cope with trauma as well as everyday life" (p. 26).

At the school-wide level, there are a number of factors that contribute to student safety and that provide boundaries for all students (Brown, 2008), including:

- The school grounds and building are safe and secure.

- The staff clearly articulates and implements behavioral expectations and procedures.

- Family members are welcomed as partners in their children's education and can communicate directly with the school staff and members.

- School staff models pro-social behaviors, including kindness and respect for others.

- Bilingual personnel are available who understand the cultures of the students and who have connections to the families.

Having a Support System in Place before a Crisis Occurs and Plans for the Unexpected

Students reacting to a memory of a traumatic event may manifest fear or frustration in a manner that may be extremely disruptive to the classroom and require immediate intervention. That intervention may be as simple as temporarily moving the student to a different classroom or as dramatic as needing assistance from outside the school to help the student calm down and regain control. Each school needs to have a plan in place for how to handle situations that are beyond the ability of the classroom teacher to regulate. Sometimes these plans are made at the building level, and at other times they are made at the district level, but foresight and preparation are essential to avoid chaos and protect both the students and the staff.

Recognizing the Types of Events That May Trigger Students

A **trigger** is "any stimulus that acts as a reminder of past overwhelming experiences and leads to the same set of behaviors or emotions that originally developed as an attempt to cope with that experience" (Wolpow et al., 2009, p. 86). Triggers may be external such as sights, sounds, or touches. They may also be internal, such as anxiety, fear, loneliness, or stress. How do we know when a trigger has been activated? By watching the students closely and getting to know their various reactions to events. When a reaction is not typical (too little or too much), it may have been a reaction to a trigger. We may need to monitor for possible triggers and prepare the student when we can. For example, telling students in advance that there will be a fire drill at 10 o'clock and explaining that the whole school will be going outside quickly and quietly and then coming back inside can help limit triggers. We should remove the trigger if possible or make it less threatening. We may need downplay a student's over-reaction as if it was not an unusual event while trying to calm the rest of the class to avoid embarrassing one student. And we may need to work with the affected student to create a plan for dealing with future situations that is acceptable and less disruptive.

Triggers can lead students to exhibit anxiety and to react in sudden and unexpected ways. According to a researcher at the Child Mind Institute (Ravitz, 2019), "Anxiety manifests in a surprising variety of ways in part because it is based on a physiological response to a threat in the environment, a response that maximizes the body's ability to either face danger or escape danger. So, while some children exhibit anxiety by shrinking from situations or objects that trigger fears, some react with an overwhelming need to break out of an uncomfortable situation. That behavior, which can be unmanageable, is often misread as anger or opposition" (p. 2).

One suggestion, based on the actions of one school we know, is to ask the teachers to list the types of events and situations that they had observed that seemed to have triggered their elementary students, the vast majority of whom were L2 students. At a staff meeting, the school then discussed how to eliminate as many of these triggers as possible and how to best ameliorate their effects if they could not be controlled. The most common triggers listed were disruptions to routines, looks or words that were considered disrespectful (whether from peers or adults), and crowds/loud noises.

Having Knowledge of the Political Situations of Students' Countries

Many teachers unfamiliar with L2 students may feel that it is not their responsibility to understand the cultural and religious backgrounds of their students or they may view this expectation as intrusive or too extreme, but most ESL or bilingual professionals have learned quickly how important this information is to a deeper understanding of their students. Teachers are conditioned to not ask students what may seem personal questions about religion or culture, but for L2 students this knowledge may prevent unnecessary problems concerning dietary restrictions, family expectations, attendance issues, and/or dress. Issues in the home country may be causing anxiety and stress in the family and could easily carry over to the classroom. Schools with large populations of students from a certain country or culture are especially vulnerable to issues if this type of information is not common knowledge to all staff members. Bilingual and bicultural staff members can be invaluable sources of such information.

It is also important to know which culture or religious groups bring with them into the classroom a history of conflict with a rival group. It is unrealistic to expect students to not be influenced by what they have seen or heard from the adults in their community. Students need to understand that these rivalries will not be tolerated, without choosing sides or allowing students to think that their feelings are unimportant. For example, one author witnessed a physical fight between two exemplary high school girls, one from Japan and one from South Korea, which stemmed from resentment between the two countries dating back to World War II.

Focusing on the Social, Emotional, and Academic Needs

The TESOL International Association (2018) published *The 6 Principles for Exemplary Teaching of English Learners,* in which the first and foundational principle is Know Your Learners. In today's student-centered classrooms, teachers are expected not to just know each students' level of academic knowledge about the specific subject being taught but to really *know* their students. This involves having a deeper relationship, beyond the basics of What's your name? and Where do you sit in my classroom? Really understanding students includes knowing their family situations, the educational backgrounds, and their learning styles. An excellent resource for this type of information is *Understanding Your Refugee and Immigrant Students: An Educational, Cultural, and Linguistic Guide* by Jeffra Flaitz (2006).

Several studies have found that the quality of teacher-student interactions is one of the most important predictors of student academic performance and adjustment (Hamre & Pianta, 2007; Mashburn & Pianta, 2006). According to the Collaborative for Academic, Social, and Emotional Learning (CASEL), "Students who report feeling listened to by teachers, involved in decisions that affect their lives, provided with opportunities to exert autonomy, and accepted by peers are more motivated and perform better in school than those who lack these positive experiences. . . .In schools characterized by supportive relationships, common goals and norms, and a sense of collaboration, students perform better academically and have fewer behavior problems" (2015, p. 9).

Another reason the student-teacher relationship is so critical is the role it plays in helping a student to overcome trauma. According to Alan Ravitz in "How to Foster Resilience in Kids" (2019, p. 1), "A child's response to a disturbing experience depends not only on his [sic] temperament and what's happened to him in the past, but on what happens *after* the experience—the kind of support he gets from his environment. If he has an effective support system, he has a good chance of recovering from the trauma. If he has an ineffective support system, or no support system at all, his chances are much worse." As shown in Chapter 1, for many children an important component of this support system is the teacher and the school.

Ravitz, in an article written for the Child Mind Institute, an organization that focuses on providing resources to help students who have experienced trauma, states that the support system of the child is critical to healing and developing resilience. He believes that if a child has "an effective support system, that child has a good chance of recovering from the trauma. If he [sic] has an ineffective support system, or no support system at all, his chances are much worse." Ravitz (2019) continues by saying that "communities are the things that make a difference. Communities include parents, siblings, teachers, friends, and other peers" (p. 1). The role of a sensitive, caring teacher cannot be overstated in helping any child, including L2 students who have experienced trauma in their lives. This caring teacher may be the bridge between schools who have not included the parents or the community because of language or cultural differences and the families who may be reluctant to include the school because they are afraid to ask for help.

What Role Do Standards Play in a Trauma-Sensitive School?

Social-emotional learning (SEL) "is the process through which children and adults acquire and effectively apply the knowledge, attitudes, and skills necessary to understand and manage emotions, set and achieve goals, feel and show empathy for others, establish and maintain positive relationships, and make responsible decisions" (CASEL, 2015, p. 5). The Collaborative for Academic, Social, and Emotional Learning (CASEL) studies schools and school districts that implement social and emotional standards and rates their effectiveness. It shares the most innovative programs and practices with the hope that these exemplars will serve as models for other districts in published guides that highlight both elementary and secondary schools that best exemplify safe and welcoming environments. CASEL's website (casel.org) has links to the social and emotional learning standards of several school districts across the country, including a Spanish version from at least one district. It also has information on several "model schools" that have implemented these practices.

Many states have begun to develop SEL standards and are expecting or requiring local districts to incorporate them into the curriculum. Some of these SEL standards are blended into the academic standards of the state, while others serve as stand-alone guidelines for school districts. The Aspen Institute (2018) has been studying the role of these standards in the learning process and has published a preliminary report in *How Learning Happens*. This report lists these as the key principles for how people learn:

- Learning is both social and emotional.
- Supporting students' social and emotional development encompasses a range of instructional approaches that must be implemented intentionally.
- The interconnectedness of social, emotional, and academic development must be reflected in all aspects of schooling.
- Effective social and emotional development creates learning environments that support each student's individual needs.
- Educators' social and emotional competence is crucial to this work.
- Local communities need to shape and drive the process of comprehensively supporting students. (pp. 10–12)

A few months later, the Aspen Institute published a more comprehensive look that included extensive reviews of academic research, visits to various classrooms and school districts, and numerous discussions with leaders in the education field. The reports states that:

> . . . integrating social, emotional, and academic development enables all students to work together well to achieve the goals of the classroom, while appreciating and respecting interpersonal differences. Social and emotional learning is sometimes regarded too narrowly as a targeted intervention just for students who experienced trauma or who have behavior issues or other special needs. Although the integration of social, emotional, and academic learning does benefit students who are confronting challenges, this integrated approach is for all students. This reality shifts the emphasis from addressing particular students' behavior or motivation to understanding the central role of the learning environment. *By not viewing students as the problem*, this approach directs adults to explore the broader environmental and social context in which students learn. (Berman, Chaffee & Sarmiento, 2018, p. 7, emphasis added)

So how does this relate specifically to English learners and the culturally and linguistically diverse student? The later Aspen Institute report answers this question by explaining that fostering an inclusive and welcoming environment helps all students, promoting:

> . . . learning opportunities that are inclusive of and responsive to the diversity of interests, aptitudes, perspectives, races, and cultures represented in the classroom. Enabling students to feel respected for their cultural identities and perspectives and to learn culturally relevant material is an essential element in creating safe, affirming, and inclusive classrooms. For example, various cultures approach social situations differently. Drawing out and valuing this diversity acknowledges students' cultures while promoting equity and expanding choices and opportunities for all students. Open conversations about culture and cultural experiences teach students to appreciate the perspective of others and the richness that diversity brings to learning. (Berman, Chaffee, & Sarmiento, 2018, pp. 7–8)

Culturally diverse students will be more willing to express their needs and concerns in this type of environment and are, therefore, more likely to be open to the types of activities and supports that can lead to healing and resilience.

Although the SEL standards were not developed specifically with English learners in mind, they certainly relate to the issues that many of these students deal with on a daily basis: They work to keep the focus on the inner child and to understanding how the emotional state of a child is critical to the learning process. These standards also remind us of the role of the teacher in the overall development of our children. Hertel and Johnson (2013) say that "as educators, we also serve as relationship coaches for our students. The relationships we establish with and among students influence the tone and demeanor in our classrooms. But even more than that, many students are keen observers of how adults relate to others in their world, so we become role models in terms of how we interact with others. Take advantage of opportunities to provide meaningful feedback when helping a student reframe an interaction that has not gone well. In many circumstances, the school may be the only opportunity for shaping healthy interactions with others" (p. 32). For so many English learners, it is the ESL or bilingual teacher who serves as a cultural interpreter, helping students bridge the cultural norms of their home and ethnic community with that of the school and the new society in which they find themselves.

While most educators understand how important it is to be sensitive to the social and emotional needs of their students, it can be complicated by the fact that so often teachers are overwhelmed with the variety and depth of problems that students bring with them to school. One recommendation for providing extra support to classroom teachers comes jointly from the ASCD and the CDC who believe that a program they call the "Whole School, Whole Community, Whole Child" model is the next evolution of the traditional coordinated school health approach. This model was launched in spring 2014 with the intention of aligning the policies, processes, and practices of the fields of education, public health, and school health (ASCD, 2014). It is based on five Whole Child tenets, originally published by ASCD in 2007 and updated in 2020:

1. Each student enters school healthy and learns about and practices a healthy lifestyle.
2. Each student learns in an environment that is physically and emotionally safe for students and adults.
3. Each student is actively engaged in learning and is connected to the school and broader community.

4. Each student has access to personalized learning and is supported by qualified, caring adults.

5. Each student is challenged academically and prepared for success in college or further study and for employment and participation in a global environment.

These five key elements emphasize how physical and emotional safety are equal to academics in the growth and maturity of a child. Creating an environment that is physically and emotionally safe is primarily the responsibility of the classroom teacher. Most of the characteristics of a trauma-sensitive teacher previously mentioned are key to ensuring that this safe environment exists and that all students can focus on the academic lesson rather than being distracted by internal or external issues. While the idea of adding more to the plate of the classroom teacher may seem overwhelming and self-defeating, it may actually provide more time if it decreases the time spent on dealing with student behavior. Most of these characteristics are a mindset, not an extra activity.

There are other benefits to classrooms that consider the needs of the students beyond academics. Students actually learn how to be more sensitive and caring to each other, and even how to take better care of themselves. CASEL (2012) found five competencies that students develop when social and emotional learning standards are implemented:

- *Self-awareness:* The ability to accurately recognize one's emotions and thoughts and their influence on behavior. This includes accurately assessing one's strengths and limitations and possessing a well-grounded sense of confidence and optimism.

- *Self-management:* The ability to regulate one's emotions, thoughts, and behaviors effectively in different situations. This includes managing stress, controlling impulses, motivating oneself, and setting and working toward achieving personal and academic goals.

- *Social awareness:* The ability to take the perspective of and empathize with others from diverse backgrounds and cultures, to understand social and ethical norms for behavior, and to recognize family, school, and community resources and supports.

- ■ *Relationship skills:* The ability to establish and maintain healthy and rewarding relationships with diverse individuals and groups. This includes communicating clearly, listening actively, cooperating, resisting inappropriate social pressure, negotiating conflict constructively, and seeking and offering help when needed.

- ■ *Responsible decision-making:* The ability to make constructive and respectful choices about personal behavior and social interactions based on consideration of ethical standards, safety concerns, social norms, the realistic evaluation of consequences of various actions, and the well-being of self and others.

When students can see into and beyond themselves and into the lives of others, they will spend less time focused on their own issues. It is the benefit of social awareness that is the most applicable to supporting English learners because one of the difficulties for culturally diverse populations is the feeling that because they may be different from others in the class, they may feel that no one really understands or cares about their situation. While having caring adults is absolutely critical to their healing, it is equally critical to have peers who are not judgmental and who genuinely care.

One aspect of social awareness is emotional intelligence, which involves recognizing and understanding the emotions of ourselves and others. It is important to realize that how people express their emotions is based in part on cultural norms and may differ from your own. Understanding the basic beliefs of the various cultures represented in a classroom can prevent misunderstandings and help bridge communication gaps.

While no teacher can know all the nuances of every culture, watching students' reactions to certain events can help prevent problems in the future. For example, Somali students may get very offended by a teacher asking a student to come to the front of the room by crooking the finger. In their culture, this gesture is used to call a dog, while moving the whole hand downward in a beckoning motion is acceptable. Simply asking the students what is offensive is the simplest way to avoid problems, especially for secondary students. Using bilingual and bicultural personnel or having community members share their culture with school personnel is especially beneficial with elementary children who may not yet be able to express why some actions upset them or be able to offer acceptable alternatives.

How Can We Train Educators to Be More Trauma-Sensitive and Promote Sensitivity and Empathy?

At a recent presentation at the International TESOL Convention, this statement was shared by Jenna Altherr Flores, a researcher in the area of refugee and immigrant trauma:

> Teachers are nervous about how to best help students who have experienced trauma. They don't feel sufficiently knowledgeable about the subject and how to best support students. She shared this concern voiced by a teacher in her program: "We aren't trained therapists or mental health professionals, so we can't do anything in the classroom" (Altherr Flores, 2018).

For educators to be the support network that students need, they must realize the value of their role with the students and also realize what they are not expected to do. For example, they are not expected to take the role of counselor or therapist, but they can show compassion and caring. Demonstrating empathy for their students and genuinely wanting to help is exactly what trauma-affected students need most.

What exactly is **empathy**? Do all teachers have empathy as part of their toolkit? How can we develop a higher level of empathy? In *Educational Leadership*, Michele Borba (2018) wrote about the "Nine Competencies for Teaching Empathy"; she says that empathy is "the foundation of a safe, caring and inclusive learning climate" (p. 23). She makes a case for the value of empathy by the teacher and explains how the teacher can influence the students to build their level of empathy as well. Students with high levels of empathy, she believes, are more engaged in the classroom, have higher academic achievement, and are better able to communicate.

However, to teach empathy to students, one must first have empathy. Leading by example is the foundation of teaching empathy to others. Some of the key competencies students need to learn are:

- Being able to read the emotional state of others.
- Looking at situations through multiple perspectives.
- Practicing kindness.

- ■ Being able to regulate their own emotions.
- ■ Having the moral courage to stand up for others in difficult situations.

Developing empathy, Borba (2018) believes, will help students "live one essential truth: *We are all humans who share the same fears and concerns, and we deserve to be treated with dignity*" (p. 28, emphasis in original).

Although demonstrating empathy for others is one aspect of the social and emotional competence that teachers need to support traumatized students, it is not enough. Teachers also need training in how best to assist students who are dealing with emotional issues, how to identify the actions that are actually cries for help, and how to know when a situation is beyond their ability to regulate in the classroom setting.

According to an article in *Education Leadership*, 20 percent of all students live with mental health issues (Merz, 2017/2018). Merz recommended that, because up to one-fifth of the students in a classroom need emotional support, teachers should be given basic training in how best to assist students with mental health issues in the classroom, as well as information on the legal and ethical implications for providing (or not providing) support. These implications will vary by state, so the training needs to be specific to the local district. The article stresses that any training needs to provide knowledge and awareness, but not the expectation that teachers become mental health experts or practitioners.

Merz (2017/2018) lists these as the topics that should be addressed with educators:

- ■ What mental health issues may a teacher realistically experience in a classroom?
- ■ How may some mental health issues be expressed in the classroom?
- ■ When should clinical language be used as a descriptor and when should it be left to mental health professionals?
- ■ What risk factors and behaviors should be seen as warning signs to signal referrals?
- ■ How can teachers make their classroom environments more accommodating for students who are at risk?

- How can teachers best assist students while protecting their own legal rights and privacy?

- What do teachers legally have to report? Who in the school is listed as a mandated reporter?

- What resources are available in the school, the district, and the community to support the educational professional and the students?

It is also important to remember that it is not just the teachers who will be interacting with children. Creating a trauma-sensitive school requires the assistance of everyone—the administrative assistants, the classroom aides, the school nurse, counselors, other students, and administrators. These individuals are also important in the critical piece of developing relationships with students and may sometimes be the person with whom some students feel the most comfortable sharing. They need training as well that is tailored to the types of interactions these people will have with children.

Developing the skills and empathy of the entire staff will be beneficial to more than just the students; it makes a more peaceful and welcoming environment for the adults in the building as well: "Every school community includes staff engaged in nonteaching roles, such as custodians, coaches, security staff, office staff, and others. They, too, are often deeply engaged with and concerned about working with students living with trauma, violence, and chronic stress and have varying degrees of confidence and support in doing so" (Zacarian, Alvarez-Ortiz, & Haynes, 2017, p. 138).

How Can We Create a Trauma-Sensitive Classroom for Immigrants?

One way we do this is addressed in *The 6 Principles for Exemplary Teaching of English Learners* (TESOL International Association, 2018). The first principle, Know the Learner, has already been discussed. The second principle is Create Conditions for Language Learning. The authors state that one method for creating this optimal condition is through the practice of teachers promoting "an emotionally positive and organized classroom, with attention to reducing students' anxiety and developing trust"

(p. 40). Naturally, until English learners feel comfortable and welcome, they will not be able to focus on academic progress, including language learning.

This principle is based on the assumption that for children to be ready to learn and to receive the maximum benefit from instruction, their basic needs must first be met. The idea of the importance of needs being met is, of course, related to Maslow's (1943) "hierarchy of needs." As you will recall, for a person to reach their potential (or the level of **self-actualization**), they must first have their basic needs met. Basic needs are physiological needs such as food, water, shelter, etc., and safety needs. When it comes to some students, meeting their basic safety needs will require that teachers know as much as is realistically possible about the "unique stresses faced by this population of students which sometimes includes a history of potentially traumatic experiences. Emphasis is placed on creating compassionate learning environments that facilitate relationships with peers, while at the same time providing intensive support for learning English, developing academic skills and content knowledge, and adjusting to life in the United States" (Craig, 2017, p. 25). While at first glance this may seem like an impossible task and beyond the scope of the classroom, Craig (2017) believes in the ability of the teacher to adequately support these children with some basic strategies: "Teachers are most successful with traumatized youth when they are able to establish themselves as a source of comfort and a secure base for exploration and learning. They establish this sense of connection by creating a relationship that reflects a balance of support and opportunity. They build teens' self-esteem by holding them to high expectations while providing the necessary scaffolds to guarantee success. . . .With enough support, youth learn how to navigate around obstacles and display adequate persistence in the face of difficulty" (p. 75).

In addition to the obvious psychological benefit of providing assistance and support to children who have experienced trauma, when it comes to English learners, there is also the added problem that trauma can actually impact a person's ability to learn a language. Louise El Yaafouri (2018), states that **transition shock**—"an umbrella term that incorporates culture shock, chronic stress, traumatic upset, and post-traumatic stress disorder—can impact student success in a number of behavioral, emotional, and physiological ways. It can also impair students' ability to acquire and make sense of a language, meaning that it creates unique challenges for America's fastest-growing student population, English language learners (ELLs), especially those students who have come from areas experiencing war or large-scale resettlement" (p. 1).

As teachers we must recognize that though the list of stressors that many immigrant children have faced and may still be facing is extensive, we cannot focus on the child's past. Those events and situations are beyond change, but teachers can assist students as they adjust to their new home, their new culture, and, for most, a new, complicated language with innumerable rules. We need to focus instead on what the child can do. Students possess an inner strength, a linguistic and cultural heritage, and a determination to succeed. Helping students to build on those assets for the next phase of their lives is the role of the trauma-sensitive teacher.

Helping students to acknowledge and tap into these assets requires a level of trust that takes time to develop, but most experts in trauma in children believe that it is a critical component in helping students move beyond their pain: "Opportunities to bond with teachers and peers, as well as the chance to discover their own competency and self-worth, help traumatized youth move beyond their past toward future achievements and success" (Craig, 2017, p. 88). Morland et al. (2013) state that "there is growing evidence that protective factors and processes such as supportive relationships with teachers, peers, family, and the community can help mediate these [mental and physical health-related] risks, resulting in improved academic performance of even the most vulnerable immigrant children over time" (p. 59). There is no special training or resources involved in creating caring, supportive relationships between school personnel and the children placed in their care for hours each day.

One final component to helping students deal with trauma is addressing peer relationships. Supportive relationships are not just between children and adults, but also between the children themselves. Birman (2002), a leader in the field of refugees and trauma, recommends that schools address discrimination that may occur between immigrants and native-born students and specifically teach conflict resolution to both groups to minimize bullying.

A Growth Mindset, an Assets-Based Approach, and Grit in the Trauma-Sensitive Classroom

Three hot topics in education that relate to SEL and trauma-informed teaching are the ideas of **growth mindset,** using an assets-based approach with students, and **grit**. Each of these concepts asks teachers and students to look at how their belief of how a person learns and how the role of their own thinking about learning impacts a person's ability to succeed. Educators sometimes refer to the term *metacognition* to discuss thinking about our own or others thinking. In each of these theories, the teacher must believe that all students can learn and succeed, and it is equally, if not more, important for students to believe it themselves.

Growth mindset is believing that students can succeed when taught to believe in their own abilities and to embrace the challenges and complexities of learning (Dweck, 2015). Trauma-affected students often feel defeated and overwhelmed with life and school, so the teacher must encourage, inspire, and show faith in the student to make the correct choices and to continue on the road to recovery and resilience (Zacarian, Alvarez-Ortiz, & Haynes, 2017).

In *Teaching to Strengths: Supporting Students Living with Trauma, Violence, and Chronic Stress*, Zacarian, Alvarez-Ortiz, and Haynes (2017) encourage educators to "focus on strengths and potential, and not pity and low expectations" (p. 19). This *assets-based approach* encourages teachers to look at what students can do, not focus on what they have not yet achieved. Because of the language and cultural differences of immigrant students, it is too easy to overlook the strengths and assets that these students bring to the classroom, and the skills that have enabled them to persevere in the face of numerous challenges: "When we allow ourselves to be influenced and changed by different perspectives and when we see these as strengths rather than obstacles, we embrace a growth mindset and in turn begin working toward a transformation model on behalf of our students" (Zacarian, Alvarez-Ortiz, & Haynes, 2017, p. 19).

A similar educational buzzword popular today is *grit*. The term denotes struggle and perseverance, despite overwhelming odds. In education, it is the concept of using personal determination to push through a difficult problem or situation to reach a desired goal. While assets-based teaching is focused on how the teacher views the student, grit is something internal on the part of the student. The teacher can assist in the role of encourager, but it is the student who has to channel this inner desire to achieve. Angela Duckworth, one of the foremost experts on grit, in an interview recorded in *Educational Leadership*, says that what she considers true grit comes from what she calls "interpersonal character strength," which she defines as "gratitude, empathy, honesty, and social and emotional intelligence—all the things that help you to get along and contribute to the lives of other people" (McKibben, 2018, p. 40).

Another expert in the area of grit is an immigrant himself. In his autobiography, Mawi Asgedom (2016) tells about how his father pushed him to succeed against seemingly impossible odds; he has used his personal experience as an immigrant from Ethiopia to motivate thousands of students, both immigrants and native-born students, to push themselves to move beyond where society expects them to go and reach their full potential. He urges students to see barriers as temporary and to look at life in two categories: what I can do now and what I will be able to do in the future. He says that "the line between the two is where you need to apply your grit" (p. 57). Many English learners have similar stories—parents, siblings, and family members who encourage and motivate students to push through difficulties and frustration and to continue to move forward. Often immigrants live in communal societies who help each other through problems and provide the impetus to push through barriers together as a form of community grit.

Assessing Teachers' Sensitivity to Trauma

As a teacher, how can you ensure that you are being sensitive to your students' needs? A self-assessment checklist of social and emotional knowledge and skills is provided in Figure 2.1. It is a shortened adaption of the self-assessment tool found on the CASEL website entitled Personal Assessment and Reflection—SEL Competencies for School Leaders, Staff and Adults. Rate yourself on your social and emotional competencies.

FIGURE 2.1

A Checklist of SEL Competencies

Social and Emotional Competency	Sometimes	Rarely	Never
I can recognize the relationship between my own emotions and how I react to others at any given time.			
I know my own biases and how they impact my view of others.			
I generally stay calm under pressure.			
I am positive most of the time and accept events I cannot change.			
I balance my work life with my personal life most of the time.			
I appreciate and work well with people from diverse backgrounds and values.			
I foster an emotionally nurturing environment in my classroom.			
I accept and give constructive feedback in a positive manner.			
I work well in a team atmosphere.			
I treat others in the way that I would like to be treated.			

Source: This self-assessment tool was independently adapted by the University of Michigan Press (copyright © 2021) from the Collaborative for Academic, Social, and Emotional Learning. Original Source: ©2017 CASEL. All rights reserved. www.casel.org

For Further Study

Alone or with colleagues in your own educational setting, consider one or all of these questions. Expanding on your learning, these questions help you plan for change from learning more about one student to focusing on changes within a program or school.

1. As an individual or together with your staff, take the trauma-sensitive educator survey. For an individual, reflect on your scores and determine areas of strength and areas in which you feel you could improve. If you are taking the survey with colleagues, discuss the results with specific considerations for how to become more sensitive in the future. Make a plan for how you or your staff could become more trauma sensitive.

2. Think of one student who was a behavior problem this year, and then consider how looking at that student through a "trauma-sensitive lens" might have made a difference.

3. Check out the CASEL website (casel.org) and find standards for your state or from a school similar to your own. How could these standards be implemented in your school?

4. What does your school do to promote social awareness for the students? How do you build this skill with your students?

5. What type of training have you had to better help you support your English learners who have experienced trauma? What other types of training do you think you need?

6. Does your school have any special programming for new arrivals or SLIFE learners to assist with transition shock? If not, what could you do to help provide assistance to this population?

7. Complete the form in Figure 2.2 based on Principle 1, Know the Learner, from *The 6 Principles for Exemplary Teaching of English Learners®: Grades K–12* (TESOL International Association, 2018). Discuss with a fellow staff member how the results of this form could help you become more empathetic.

FIGURE **2.2**

Checklist for Principle 1: Know the Learner

Look at the characteristics listed based on Principle 1, Know the Learner, from *The 6 Principles for Exemplary Teaching of English Learners®: Grades K–12* (2018, p. 37) and think about one English learner that you feel that you know well. Complete as much of this chart as you can about that student. Then think of a second ESL student that you did not know as well. Write what you knew about that person in the next column.

How did knowing basic information about a student impact your ability to make more informed and appropriate instructional decisions? Be specific if possible.

Basic Information	First Student	Second Student
Home country of student or family		
Home language		
Cultural background		
Level of proficiency in reading, writing, and speaking in English		
Home language literacy level		
Educational background		
Socio-emotional background		
Special needs		
Learning preferences		
Life experiences		
Gifts and talents		
Interests and life goals		
Sociopolitical context of home country		

8. Check out these additional resources for information on serving ELs with trauma backgrounds:

   ❑ National Child Traumatic Stress Network (nctsn.org). This organization provides a number of videos and programs to help schools and mental health experts deal with such issues as early childhood trauma, complex trauma, and refugee trauma.

   ❑ Child Trauma Toolkit for Educators by the National Child Traumatic Stress Network (nctsn.org). This toolkit is available for free to download for any interested parties. It includes chapters on the psychological and behavioral impact of trauma on various ages of students and also a chapter on self-care for educators.

   ❑ Refugee Health Technical Assistance Center. Refugeehealthta. org. This site has a number of research briefs and webinars on refugees and trauma, including one on refugees and suicide. www.k12.wa.us/student-success/health-safety/mental-social-behavioral-health/compassionate-schools-learning-and/heart-learning-compassion-resiliency-and-academic-success

   ❑ Wolpow, R., Johnson, M., Hertel, R., & Kincaid. S. (2009). *The heart of learning and teaching: Compassion, resilience, and academic success.* Olympia: Washington State Office of the Superintendent of Public Instruction. This extremely thorough document provides tips for educators on dealing with trauma and building resilience for all students, but much of what is included is definitely appropriate for English learners. www.k12.wa.us/student-success/health-safety/mental-social-behavioral-health/compassionate-schools-learning-and/heart-learning-compassion-resiliency-and-academic-success

   ❑ Trauma Informed Positive Behaviour Support (tipbs.com) is an organization in Australia that offers programs for schools that provide a number of supports for working with trauma-background students.

3

Instructional Strategies and Classroom Activities That Foster Resilience

---

Resilience presents a challenge for psychologists. Whether you can be said to have it or not largely depends not on any particular psychological test but on the way your life unfolds. If you are lucky enough to never experience any sort of adversity, we won't know how resilient you are. It's only when you're faced with obstacles, stress, and other environmental threats that resilience, or the lack of it, emerges: Do you succumb or do you surmount?

—McElhiney, n.d.

Resilience **is a term that,** in recent years, has been overused according to a *New York Times Magazine* essay called "The Profound Emptiness of 'Resilience'" (December 6, 2015). The essay writer indicated that *resilience* has been used in contexts from "toughening up your investment portfolio to your toddler"; she stated that *resilience*, from the Latin meaning "to jump up again," is "not just the strength to stay the course but to question it and propose to others, not just how to survive but to thrive." Beyond the foundational and somewhat generic definition, this chapter explores what psychologists and researchers have discovered helps the education practitioner foster resilience in the English learner recovering from trauma.

What Is the Research-Based Background for Identifying Resilience in At-Risk Children?

In the late 1980s, one developmental psychologist and clinician, Martin Garmezy, was struck by the behavior of one of his patients, a nine-year-old boy. Although the boy lived with an alcoholic mother and absent father, he did not want anyone to feel pity for him or know about his mother. Garmezy noted that this boy was among a cohort of children whom he identified as succeeding, if not excelling, in spite of acute circumstances. He later identified this trait as *resilience* and thus became the first to label and study this concept (Masten, Best, & Garmezy, 1990).

In another study, developmental psychologists Werner and Smith (2001) found that one of the factors that set resilient children apart from other at-risk children in their study was how children responded to their environment. Similarly to Garmezy, they noted how their subjects were able "to meet the world on their own terms" (p. 57). The resilient children in their study felt that they were in control of their own circumstances, achievements, and successes and saw themselves as what Konnikova (2016) referred to as "orchestrators of their own fate."

Werner and Smith (2001) also noted that one-third of the 698 children in Kauai that they studied never seemed to be affected by grinding poverty, alcoholism, and/or abuse in the homes in which they grew up. Instead, resilience developed in spite of the challenges they faced. These children maintained their self-esteem, and the continued positive responses to the adversity they faced over time became, as what Mirano (2003) observed, "incorporated into their inner selves as lasting strengths."

In addition, George Bonanno, a clinical psychologist at Columbia University, has been studying resilience since 1991. His focus has been on why and how some people are better at dealing with adversity. He believes that all people have the same fundamental stress-response systems, but his research shows that some people are able to use the system more effectively than others, enabling them to become resilient to adversity, trauma, and setbacks. His research shows that the way that someone conceptualizes an event makes all the difference: if the event is viewed as traumatic, there is a negative response, which makes the person more vulnerable. But Bonanno (2004) indicates those who exhibit self-confidence in their ability to cope and have a sense of optimism often feel they are able to deal with adversity.

All of these researchers helped shift the thinking forward to the positive. The work of earlier researchers "looked at areas of vulnerability, investigating the experiences that make people susceptible to poor life outcomes, rather than focused on areas of young learner strengths to reframe a negative situation" (Konnikova, 2016). Because of the importance of resilience to our students, we will use the positive work as a foundation for the classroom activities specifically designed to build resilience in English learners.

How Can We Help Build Resilience in Immigrant Children?

This chapter focuses on building and supporting the strengths of the immigrant student in the classroom and how to help these learners feel that they have a place in the school community, a place where they can explore who they are, recognize their strengths, and secure supports when needed, as well as look positively toward their futures—in essence, to become resilient learners.

Our previous book (Custodio & O'Loughlin, 2017), featured the work of Edith Grotberg (1995) and her "I Have, I Am, I Can" specifically, as a way to foster resilience in SLIFE learners. Again, her work has an important role to play for immigrant and refugee students.

Grotberg's research (1995) demonstrated her belief that each child has strengths that they bring with them to every situation in their lives. For her, resilience is the **universal capacity** that every person has to minimize or overcome the damaging effects of adversity. She has labeled the three sources of resilience as "I Have, I Am, and I Can." We will apply these labels to the rest of this chapter and will identify the audience for, focus of, and ways of implementing each activity for denoting how each could work with specific age/grade groups of English learners. Some of these activities will be labeled as appropriate for newcomers or SLIFE. Many of these students will have beginning levels of English and may require additional supports to access the activities. (See the Introduction for more on these particular populations.)

Using the "I Have, I Am, and I Can" Model to Foster Resilience

I Have

According to Grotberg (1995), "I Have" means that children feel that:

- I am surrounded by people I can trust and who believe in me.

- I have people who will set limits for me.

- I have people who will support my learning and especially help me to work toward learning on my own.

- I have people who are there for me when I am sick, in danger, worried, or need support to learn.

One "I Have" classroom procedure that will help learners move from trauma to resilience is the use of **morning meetings.** Morning meetings help all students feel that they are part of the classroom community and can become a time of relationship-building. Minero (2017) and Thomas (2018) recommend that all grades could benefit from starting the day with a morning meeting, not just elementary grades. The goals of morning meeting should include merging social interactional skills and academic learning through open conversation. These meetings typically last 10–15 minutes. (Edutopia offers several other resources on morning meetings including some video clips.)

Morning meetings set the tone for the day of instruction and bring together learners who would otherwise go directly to a class without connecting to the community of other immigrant students; this type of connection improves student well-being. Morning meetings also address Principle 2 of *The 6 Principles for Exemplary Teaching of English Learners,* which promotes "an emotionally positive and organized classroom with attention to reducing students' anxiety and developing trust" (TESOL International Association, 2018, p. 40).

Morning Meeting

Grade Levels: All

Language Development Levels: All levels

Implementation Suggestions:

1. Require master scheduling for morning and end-of-day meeting times and dedicated space for middle and high school English learners.

2. Differentiate with visuals, sentence stems/frames, and adjusted speech for lower levels.

Choosing a gathering place within the classroom is important so that all students share the space and can see one another and the teacher. This is usually accomplished with a focal point, an open space available for all students to sit comfortably on the floor or in chairs, facing the teacher.

As students enter the classroom and before beginning the daily morning meeting, we ask learners to respond to a **mood meter** (see Figure 3.1) or a "how are you feeling" prompt? This can be done in many verbal and non-verbal ways. Young learners can tap one of three colors on a traffic light where green means "good to go," yellow means "some minor things are worrying me," and red means "I am feeling really stressed." Older learners can identify publicly or privately (just between the student and teacher) a place on a mood meter graphic that has four quadrants colored red, yellow, blue, or green and labeled with phrases such as *anxious/worried/annoyed* (red); *calm/peaceful/comfortable* (green); *happy/pleased/proud* (yellow); and *sad/lonely/discouraged* (blue). Wording for the four quadrants is adjusted to meet the vocabulary ability level of the learners and can also be represented with icons or colors alone (Brackett, 2018). Students can cross quadrants to indicate a combination of feelings.

FIGURE **3.1**

Example of Mood Meter

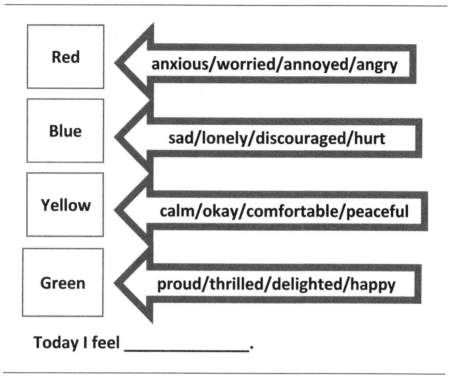

Red	anxious/worried/annoyed/angry
Blue	sad/lonely/discouraged/hurt
Yellow	calm/okay/comfortable/peaceful
Green	proud/thrilled/delighted/happy

Today I feel _____.

A morning meeting usually consists of these three components:

1. Beginning the Meeting

- Students quietly move to the meeting place, greet one another, and await the teacher's agenda for the meeting.

- The teacher presents the agenda for the meeting orally, as well as visually for SLIFE, with bulleted words/ phrases and pictures or icons, as needed. (SLIFE are students with years of missing education who may need extra support throughout the day.)

- The teacher makes announcements about the learning activities for the day (elementary) or for the class (secondary), as well as any schoolwide announcements (e.g., assemblies, schedule changes, lunch or bus procedures, etc.).

- Students share ideas and/or ask questions. This sharing can happen in various ways—as a full class or pair-share, for example. The topic for sharing can be a teacher-chosen one or a free-choice one. Students ask questions of their classmates during a free-choice share. Practicing how to ask appropriate questions is part of the experience, and for immigrant students sentence stems and sentence frame prompts can be put on index cards, a word wall, in their notebooks, etc.

- Students can share with the whole group if appropriate.

2. Creating an Individual or Group Activity

Create a group activity to bring closure to the morning meeting, moving into the school day/academic instruction with positive energy. Suggested activities could include a choral recitation, such as a poem (from a present or past unit of instruction) or an excerpt from a shared class story or song. It could also include something individualized such as one of these options:

- *Talk to Yourself:* Sit silently and think about your day ahead. Tell yourself with positive words that today will be a good day. Some immigrant learners may need native language and English paired words on flashcards. Flash cards should be prepared in advance and always available to the learner to use in morning meetings and other times during the day.

- *Mindful Breathing:* Sit tall, and then breathe in and out softly and slowly on the count of three with eyes closed; students should breathe in through their noses and out through their mouths, expelling any worry to begin the day.

- *Stand Up Tall:* This exercise requires visualizing and balance. As a tree, you have your feet firmly "rooted" on the floor and you imagine these are your roots going down through the floor. Keep your hands at your sides and imagine you are a tall rooted tree that can endure wind and rain. Slowly raise your arms and separate your fingers. You are a strong tree, even when the wind blows waves at your base.

More activities such as these can be found in Stewart (2017) *Mindful Kids: 50 Mindfulness Activities for Kindness, Focus, and Calm.*

3. Ending the Morning Meeting

Teachers often end the meeting with a few encouraging words about the day ahead and may repeat some of the announcements from the start of the morning meeting. Before moving to their assigned start of the academic day, students revisit the feelings traffic light/chart or mood meter and reassess their current feelings. This revisit provides the teacher with important feedback (see Figure 3.1). Morning Meetings address the "I Have" because learners realize over time that they are surrounded by other students with whom they share commonalities, who understand them, believe in them, and feel that there are others they can trust.

Mapping Your Environment

Grade Levels: All

Language Development Levels: All levels

Implementation Suggestions: Use word banks, as needed, for different levels of learners. If agreed to by English learners, maps can be shared in a public place within the school (see Chapter 5) as part of the recognition and validation of the diversity of students.

Students should consider: What resources are available to me in my community? This can be especially beneficial for new arrivals and SLIFE, helping them to "map" their environments. It helps them to know what and whom they have who can help them. The map acts like a living mural. Students can use paper posted in the classroom on which they draw a map of their community and label each person, building, street, object, and living space on the mural, adding new "I Haves" as they develop.

Photo Journaling

Grade Levels: All

Language Development Levels: All

Implementation Suggestions: For Grades K–2, students can draw their "photos" in place of using a camera, using a word bank of key words and phrases along with sentence stems. Differentiated word banks, descriptive words, and sentence stems/frames can be used by older learners as needed.

Photo journaling is another tool to use to describe visually what and who immigrant students have as supports, not only for their learning, but also for their sociocultural interactions and supports from teachers, classmates, family, and other community members. 100 Cameras, described in For Further Study, includes activities for using cameras to document student experiences. There are excellent suggestions on the website for creating student-led visual narrative projects and for learners to tell their unique story.

Photo journaling and mapping, using visual images only or images and words, can both symbolize and help the learners recognize their support system. Mapping and photo journaling, with single word or phrase labeling, may be all that newcomers can do at this point. For more advanced learners, the two-column graphic organizer can capture what "I Have" now and what is possible in the future. Teachers can provide a word bank of phrases and sentence starters for support. From the graphic organizer to narrative, students can begin to write and reflect in present and past tense. Students choose if and when they wish to share their "I Have" journals with other learners and their teachers.

Picture Books and Other Literature

Grade Levels: All

Language Development Levels: All levels: books read to and read by learners

Implementation Suggestions: See suggested picture book selection checklist in the Appendix to determine book choices based on vocabulary, illustrations, and age-grade appropriate topics.

For young learners, there are numerous picture books that exemplify the "I Have" resources in a school and community that are part of a newcomer's support system. Although migration narratives are discussed in more detail later in the "I Am" and "I Can" sections of the chapter and organized in other categories for reading with and to students, the Appendix provides a more substantial and annotated list of picture book and other reading choices.

When carefully chosen, picture books can provide moments in time to explore what other newcomers, regardless of age, have faced emigrating to a new country and what "I Haves" helped them persevere and acculturate. Story plotlines begin with how the journey has taken them to a new, unfamiliar environment, with cultural miscues, limited language to express feelings and needs, and how the support of others, whether classmates, teachers, or supportive parents helped the newcomer.

A few examples for elementary and secondary students are listed here. See the Appendix for additional titles.

- *My Name is Sangoel* (Karen Williams). Sangoel comes to the U.S. with his mother and sister. His father has died in the war in the Sudan. The story follows his adjustment to his new life and home, the symbolic meaning of his name, his "I Have," and how he resolves the difficulties other find with pronouncing his name.

Two choices for older students include:

- *Of Beetles and Angels: A Boy's Remarkable Journey from a Refugee Camp to Harvard* (Mawi Asgedom). Autobiographical account of immigration.
- *A Long Walk to Water* (Linda Sue Park). Fictionalized account of Sudan.

A selection of non-fiction picture books related to perseverance and growth includes:

- *Bounce Back: A Book about Resilience* (Cheri Meiners and Elizabeth Allen). This book for primary age learners focuses on having a positive outlook and how to feel good about yourself and your life, providing ways of looking at situations in your life to be happy and contribute to others' happiness.

- *Being Me: A Kid's Guide to Boosting Self-Confidence and Self-Esteem* (Wendy Moss). The book is appropriate for learners four years and older. It empowers children to understand and recognize their self-worth and develop confidence in themselves, their abilities, and the choices they make for themselves.

- *My Name My Identity: Take the Pledge* project that started in the Santa Clara County Office of Education in Santa Clara, California: www.mynamemyidentity.org)

- *6 Strategies for Building Better Student Relationships.* Strategy 1: Learn names quickly and correctly. www.edutopia.org/article/6-strategies-building-better-student-relationships

I Am

To Grotberg (1995), "I Am" means that children feel that:

- I am a person that people can like and trust.
- I respect myself and respect others.
- I am responsible for things that I do.
- I am strong and can share my strengths with others.
- I am happy to feel empathy and show concern for others.

Migration Narratives

Grade Levels: All

Language Development Level: All levels

Implementation Suggestions: Students can draw, write, or combine drawing and writing. Students should be supplied with sentence stems/frames, word banks, or graphic organizers to tell their story.

As Joan Wink (2018) wrote in *The Power of Story*, "Stories have power. Stories matter. Stories bind us together… . Encouraging student-initiated stories tells each of them she matters/he matters; each [that] life has value; stories affirm each students' own identity (Cummins et al., 2005)" (p. 45). Expressing one's "I Am" is more than just affirming one's own identity and sharing who one is now and in the future; it can be a step toward cultural adaptation, modeling how a student has or will become strong and resilient.

Reading and writing one's own **migration narrative** can help the immigrant learners reflect on others' migration experiences in addition to sharing his/her own. Sandra Duval (2018) in *Teachers as Allies: Transformative Practices for Teaching DREAMers and Undocumented Students* states that caring adults can "diminish the impact of **toxic stress** from immigration trauma on the developing brain…by using autobiographical reflections and 'power of the story'" (p. 48).

The Migrant Children Storytelling website (migrantchildstorytelling. org) collects stories from migrant children from anywhere in the world. The migrant stories can be in words, pictures, photographs, or in a video. There are no limitations about story topics; the stories presented are specifically decided by the writer and are of importance to the child. The website indicates that it uses the term "migrant to include all children who have been forced, or have chosen, to leave their home country for any reason, and who are trying to establish a life in another country." The Migrant Child Storytelling Project is supported by a non-profit, non-governmental organization, Rights and Opportunities Foundation. The principles of the foundation include human rights and a mission for improving the world through "education, humanitarian assistance and environmental protections."

According to Scullen (2019), "Culturally relevant and inclusive texts are essential reading for newcomers" (p. 8). When students can see themselves, their own culture, and similar stories to their own reflected in the curriculum, it is empowering. Students not only relate to similar stories from others like themselves, but also see the "relevance and authenticity," for learning to read and reading to learn.

According to the Wolpow et al. (2009):

> Many teachers have found that reading literature of other trauma survivors is often well-received. Obviously, this option should be a choice, offered with the awareness that trauma literature could trigger memories that could worsen behavior or unintended withdrawal into silence. Nevertheless, teachers who have taught the Holocaust or literature about WWII internment camp picture-books (as two examples of this type of literature) to adolescents have observed that most find this reading engaging, and many are willing to share their personal responses to it in writing. What is more, many teachers recognize the power that creative writing provides as an outlet for their students. This writing can provide safe ways for students to put on paper the triggers that haunt them. (p. 25)

There are numerous "migration stories" available in both picture books for young and older learners, as well as non-fiction short stories and books for older learners. A few examples are described and a longer list will be included in the Appendix.

- *From North to South* (Rene Lainez and Joe Cepeda). The author describes the experiences of a family separated on both sides of the border between San Diego and Mexico.

- *Dia's Story Cloth: The Hmong People's Journey to Freedom* (Dia Chi). The focus of this story is on the story cloth made for the author by her aunt and uncle as she journeys to the U.S. from Laos and the symbolic meaning of the cloth.

- *The Arrival* (Shaun Tan). A wordless graphic novel in six parts that visually tells the story of a man leaving his homeland and starting a new life for himself and family.

- *Refugee* (Stan Gantz). The intertwining story of three refugee children from Nazi Germany, Castro's Cuba, and Syria.

Reading migration stories and having students reflect in writing could include telling one's own story if the learner feels comfortable doing so. In "My Journey of Hope and Peace," Stewart (2015) describes a project with high school refugees who wrote about their own refugee experience. After reading various texts, the students participated in class discussions, personal journal writing, and created graphic illustrations of their journeys.

Reading migration stories and asking students to reflect in writing could include telling one's own story if the learner feels comfortable doing so. Other alternatives to a written narrative could be drawing, painting, writing a song, or creating a short play.

Testimonial Therapy

Grade Levels: Middle/high school, adult learners

Language Development Levels: All

Implementation Suggestions: Differentiate the activity for different learner levels with visuals, sentence stems/frames, and adjusted speech for lower levels.

Testimonial therapy is a technique that has been found to be effective for older teens and adults who have experienced traumatic events. In testimonial therapy, the person either writes or orally tells the story of their migration experience. How much or how little is shared is totally up to the individual. After the narrative is complete, a small ceremony is held in which the story is read and then burned to symbolically show that the painful memories are gone, and the person is beginning a new phase of life. The ceremony often includes any family members or friends that the person personally invites to celebrate the event.

This type of therapy does not require a licensed counselor but should only be encouraged for someone who is ready for the experience and who understands what it involves (at least months or possibly even years after arrival). They can stop at any time they feel uncomfortable and resume later when they feel ready. If they chose not to hold the final ceremony, that is absolutely acceptable. This should be a voluntary experience that should be available to an individual with an interest, but never pushed on anyone. According to Wilkins (2019), Catholic Charities of Cleveland has been using testimonial therapy with interested clients in its organization for a few years and encourages other organizations to begin trying this type of therapy with other formerly traumatized immigrants.

Dialogue Journals

Grade Levels: All

Language Development Levels: All

Implementation Suggestions:

1. Set time aside during the school day schedule for all learners to write.

2. Younger ELs and newcomers can draw and/or write in native language, when able.

3. K–2 newcomers can draw and indicate through invented spelling, what they wish to express and share with the teacher and/or other ELs.

Dialogue journals allow students to share their feelings in a private way. Setting up a space in your room where students can securely keep their journals to use during a designated writing time or free reading/writing time helps them not only begin to write with fluency, expressing their questions, concerns, worries, and accomplishments. Students experiment with language and can use both English and their native language to express ideas that are difficult to address in English. The word *dialogue* indicates that teachers respond to student journal entries, with feedback on content, to praise or question an entry, and to answer a question or make suggestions, but never to correct and/or grade language use or grammar. The importance of a dialogue journal is to practice language in writing and to build fluency. It is also a tool to note when there are EL concerns and questions. Confidentiality is key to communicating with the writer.

Translanguaging

Grade Levels: Middle or high school

Language Development Levels: Learners with strong native language literacy skills

Implementation Suggestions: Speak-to-write strategies allow learners the ability to use native language to express both social and academic language, their "I Can" in speech and use both native language and English for written response.

Translanguaging, using native language to support concepts, thoughts, and feelings that are difficult to express in English, helps students more fluently express themselves (Garcia & Wei, 2014). Freeman, Freeman, and Soto (2016) believe that translanguaging, writing in both languages, helps to affirm emergent bilingual students' identities while scaffolding academic content instruction and academic language development. "From a holistic perspective," the Freemans and others believe, "bilinguals do not have two separate language systems. Instead, they have one linguistic system in which linguistic features constantly interact" (p. 19).

Finally, combining translanguaging with journal writing provide teachers with authentic language samples and a way to determine language development over time, including identifying problem areas to include in lessons. More significantly, dialogue journals allow students to communicate in a safe environment about subjects that are important to them. Even when teachers do not understand the first language of the student, dialogue journals provide the student with an outlet to freely express feelings, experiences, fears, and hopes. Translanguaging in journal entries enables students "to bring their whole selves into the classroom" (Hamman, Beck, & Donaldson, 2018) and validate their languages and cultures.

Photo or Video "Voices"

Grade Levels: All

Language Development Levels: All

Implementation Suggestions:

1. Provide sentence frames/stems for students to use when determining captions for a photo book or creating a short monologue for video.

2. Develop an example photo book and/or video to model for students.

3. K–1 learners may need to draw their "photos" and be given a single-word word bank to create captions.

Students can create their I Am narratives through photos, creating a photo book with captions, or through the creation of a video, using a smart phone or digital camera. They can enhance the story with artifacts from their cultures. This form of expression works well for students with very limited or significantly interrupted native language such as SLIFE learners. Pairs of students can work together, with one helping to create a simple narrative to create captions for the pictures.

Mural or Collage

Grade Levels: All

Language Development Levels: All

Implementation Suggestions: Provide all supplies for students, including pictures in magazines and/or online, scissors, glue, etc., and then model with think-alouds. Provide sentence frames/sentence stems and demonstrate how to connect them to the visual representation.

Students can create their own murals or collages to be displayed in the classroom. **Murals** and **collages** could be labeled with single words or short phrases in English and students' native language. This is also a good medium of expression for the more limited learners. Students can choose whether or not to display murals and collages in the classroom or other locations in the school to share their I Am with classmates. An art exhibit of student work could be displayed in the school to celebrate the diversity of learners in their new environment (see Cultural Walkthroughs in Chapter 5). Murals or collages can be accompanied by photos and a brief "About the artist," which students can write with the support of sentence stems or sentence frames, including native language titles and/or phrases describing their I Am art.

Autobiographical "I Am" Bio Cube

Grade Levels: Grades 2–5 (can be done with middle school students as well)

Language Development Levels: Beginners and higher; more difficult for newcomers

Implementation Suggestions:

1. Draft answers on a graphic organizer before placing words and illustrations on cube squares.

2. If learners have already written autobiographical text at other times, help students develop an updated "I Am" summary version of whom they have become and their current strengths.

   A **bio cube** is six-sided foldable piece of paper on which a student includes specific information in each square of the cube. Students can use the sections of the cube to write and/or draw their own "I Am" story. Bio cubes can be used throughout the school year to add to who "I Am," as well as celebrating what "I Can" do now. A suggested order of topic contents for each of the six sides to the cube could include (1) title—All about Me; (2) facts about me (birthdate, birthplace, languages I speak, family members, etc.; (3, 4, 5) important events and people in my life and my dreams for the future; and (6) a symbol that represents me labeled. Bio cube blackline masters with folding directions are available at www.readwritethink.org.

Memo and/or Letter to Self

Grade Levels: Upper elementary through high school

Language Development Levels: High-beginner through advanced

Implementation Suggestions: A memo or letter to self can celebrate who a student is now and look toward the future for more accomplishments in the future.

Menu or Recipe

Grade Levels: Upper elementary through high school

Language Development Levels: High-beginning through advanced.

Implementation Suggestions: For the menu or recipe, use with intermediate and/or advanced learners because the creating of a menu or recipe requires analogy and/or symbolism to describe oneself (e.g., an appetizer would suggest small accomplishments; a main dish could describe a major changes in language ability or abilities to express oneself and become more autonomous; a side dish could be recognizing how family, siblings, and/or friends who have influenced "I Am;" and dessert could be what each person looking forward to becoming).

Comparing yourself to a menu or recipe does not necessarily mean creating a "food" menu or recipe, but rather describing one's self with attributions (see Figure 3.2). Bilingual or picture dictionaries support the creation of a menu or recipe.

I Can

To Grotberg (1995), "I Can" means that children feel that:

- I can speak with someone about the things that frighten or worry them.
- I can problem-solve on my own or with support.
- I use self-control to stop before doing something that is wrong or could be dangerous.
- I seek help when needed, including knowing where to find help and knowing when reaching out for help is needed.

FIGURE **3.2**

Sample: My Food Identity, Culture, and Heritage

The samples here are to help begin the discussion on the connection between foods and the learner's identity. Students create their own chart of foods and what they mean to their identity. For students who are unable to write without support, help the student generate a list of favorite foods and use a sentence stem, such as: _____ is part of me, my culture, and my family because _____.

Food	What It Means to My Identity
Empanadas	My grandma made empanadas for breakfast, lunch, or a snack. If I close my eyes, I can see my grandma humming while pinching the dough into crescent shapes filled with delicious meats. The smells and tastes are part of the story of who I am.
Matzoh Ball Soup	This soup is a part of me, my culture, and my family. I remember helping my mother form the matzoh balls, cut up the carrots, and put everything together into the soup. It was part of all of our special meals for holidays. I can remember the smell, the slightly salty taste, and soft matzoh balls in my mouth. It is a time when we lit candles, said prayers over the meal, and really felt like a family.
Gyoza	Americans call these pot stickers or dumplings. Gyoza my mother made were filled with pork or shrimp or vegetables. My sister and I helped fill these half-moon dough shapes and listened to her stories of helping her mother make gyoza when she was a child. I thought about all the generations in my family who had their own special recipes for these tiny delicious treats.
Hot Dogs	Hot dogs have a special meaning in my new culture and identity. I discovered that hot dogs are not "hot" or are they "dogs." English is a funny language. Hot dogs are part of every summer party, barbeque, picnic, and even baseball games. I'm learning so much about how hot dogs bring people together to share happy events.

In "I Can," the third and final building resilient learners' component, it is important for immigrant learners to understand what they are able to accomplish on their own or with help now and what they hope to be able to do on their own in the future. Different, from the "I Have, I Can" realistically addresses their ability to problem-solve; determine self-control zones; use think-before-act tools; and appropriately seek outside help for emotional, social, and academic needs.

Creating an emotional goal-setting activity in a three-column chart (see Figure 3.3), for looking at both short- and long-term objectives, as well as brainstorming what I Can Do Now, provides a foundation for students to begin working on the goal of what I Hope I Can Do Soon.

FIGURE **3.3**
"I Can" Goals

"I Can" Goals	"I Can" Do Now	"I Can" Do in the Future
Speak with someone I trust about the things that frighten or worry me	I can write or write/ draw these now in my journal but don't feel comfortable talking about things that worry me.	I hope to be able to describe in words my worries and ask a trusted teacher for help.
Volunteer to answer a question in class	I can answer yes/no questions with single words or phrases.	I want to be able to answer *how, when,* and *where* questions in full sentences.
Problem-solve on my own or know when and how to ask for help	I can ask a teacher to repeat information I didn't understand.	I want to be able to know where to look for simple answers on my own and when I need to ask a teacher or another student for help.
Use self-control to stop before doing something that is wrong or could be dangerous; knowing when I feel this frustration or stress coming	I can, some of the time, go to the "quiet corner" and sit quietly, and wait until the anxious or angry feeling stops.	I want to be able to know how to find the signals that tell me I'm beginning to feel stress and stop.

Scattergram

A **scattergram** is a chart with a line drawn horizontally across the middle, with words, visuals, and/or clipped pictures from magazines to represent what "I Can" do now and what I hope to do in the future in social and interactional situations. The visual representation in Figure 3.4 is a variation on the scattergram, using boxes above and below the line to insert words or phrases. If needed, newcomers can make a list, which would become a word bank for use with the scattergram.

Grade Levels: Grades 4 and higher; K–3 would need many resources, including word banks, brainstorming, and modeling

Language Development Levels: High-beginner to advanced

Implementation Suggestions:

1. Use a word bank and sentence stems/frames.

2. Partners can generate more language than working alone.

3. Visuals drawn and/or from magazines or clip art websites are helpful.

For academic purposes, students could use a graphic organizer, such as a **scattergram** (see Figure 3.4), to indicate above the line what they can do now and below the line what they hope to do soon. Once students have accomplished the task, they move the icon or sentence block above the line. This both visual and tactile approach to noting what "I Can" provides both motivation and recognition of abilities. Working with a partner can encourage students to support one another in accomplishing some of the more difficult I Can academic tasks.

FIGURE **3.4**

Example of "Can Do" and "Hope to Do" Soon

Now	Can write a complete sentence. Can tell how I feel today.
Soon	Can write a complete paragraph. Can write about my experiences.

To stave off students' frustration with what they "cannot" do now, those barriers to resilience, teachers can implement some of the following to build learner confidence and address the "I Can":

■ Foster optimism and encouragement through genuine compliments specific to completion of a task, encourage risk-taking in small steps (e.g., volunteering to answer a question, performing a classroom task, working with a partner), or refocus from negative responses about tasks that did not go well to providing suggestions for how to succeed in the future.

■ Model how to practice metacognition, being aware of one's own feelings, thoughts, and actions at a given time. Help students identify their stressors. Tools such as a What Zone Are You In? chart helps students to tune into themselves and know how they are feeling at the moment, rate themselves, and look into their own toolbox to help themselves recover when feelings of frustration, anger, fear, or worry take over. This activity is similar to the before morning meeting activity and can be a follow-up later in the day, with the same or different graphic organizer tool. As mentioned earlier, students return at the end of the day to the morning meeting room and debrief, as well as check in with What Zone Are You In? This is quite helpful for teachers who can meet with a student who has had a difficult experience and/ or day at school before the learner leaves for the day. Many concerns and issues can be addressed if "caught" before the learner leaves school for the day.

Students can use sticky notes to note on a classroom color-coded chart how they are feeling at the beginning of the day.

■ Red could indicate stress, fear, or worry.
■ Yellow could indicate "I'm okay" but not feeling great.
■ Green could indicate "Today is going to be a great day."

They are then able to move the sticky note to another zone as the day goes on and ends. An end-of-day writing or drawing as a ticket out helps the teacher to be aware of student feelings for that day; then the teacher plans for a one-to-one meeting with the student to discuss potential problems. The Teachers' Pay Teachers website (www.teacher-spayteachers.com) provides numerous examples that can be replicated to meet your unique setting.

Think–Wait–Respond

Grade Levels: All – but variations exist for different grade-level clusters, such as K–2, 3–5, or 6–12.

Language Development Levels: High-Beginner to Advanced

Implementation Suggestions: K–3 may need to count down from 5-1; move an object or himself from one place to another, indicating decompressing and not getting angry; activities listed can be modeled/taught/practiced by older learners.

Model and practice wait time: Think–wait–respond to help deal with impulsivity, anxiety, and practice listening to others. These types of activities help students build on their "I Can" repertoires, noting positively how they address small stressors in their daily school life. A few tactile activities also help here:

- Drawing: Provide paper to draw how they feel in a think-wait-respond protocol. Students ask themselves: "How do I feel at the beginning and how do I feel now?" Paper can be divided into two sections or a t-chart graphic organizer can be used to show how students feel first and when they are ready to come back to the group/class.

- Coloring: Using a pre-made picture to color while decompressing before returning to the group/class.

- Tactile: Peeling an orange with eyes closed, taking time to think, feel, and experience before responding.

- Tactile: Melting an ice cube in the hand or mouth, taking deep breaths until the cube has totally melted.

Community-Building Activities for Elementary School

These activities ensure that young learners feel that they are part of the classroom community (Berger & Riojas-Cortez, 2016).

■ *Acts of Kindness*: Noticing when others have been kind to classmates; providing kindness instructions to students, such as writing an anonymous note or letter to a peer recognizing their accomplishments.

■ *Be a Friend on Friday*: Celebrate personal accomplishments, yourself and others; write an anonymous note to another student, use self-talk (note for students, sentence frames or sentence stems could be used), use storytelling resources to peer-read and talk about it. A separate list has been provided for elementary learners.

■ *Use picture books on topics of longing and empowerment*:
  □ *I Can Do Hard Things* (Gabi Garcia)
  □ *Listening with My Heart* (Gabi Garcia)
  □ *I Won't Quit* (Danny McGill)
  □ *I Can Handle It* (Laurie Wright)
  □ *I Will Be Okay* (Laurie Wright)

Community-Building Activities for Middle and High School

■ *Paper Tweets*: A template of a speech bubble is used to create a profile. Students must each have three followers—a friend, an acquaintance, and someone with whom they rarely interact. Newcomers and other students can respond to teacher prompts about their current mood, new things in their lives, and then respond to their followers, thus creating a group to which they "Can" reach out (Fletcher, 2018).

■ *Daily Closing Activity*: Students sit in a circle at the end of the day and share one appreciation idea about a peer, an apology, or a "lightbulb moment."

■ *Rose and Thorn*: Similar to the daily closing activity but at the beginning of the day. Share one rose ("I Can") and one thorn (*I am challenged by...*). Students can return to their "rose and thorn" at the end of the day or the end of the week to indicate if a "thorn" has moved into the "rose" column, validating a new "I Can."

■ Use picture books and chapter books on overcoming adversity:

☐ *Emmanuel's Dream* (Laurie Ann Thompson). This is a true story of young boy from Ghana who had one deformed leg, and only one foot, but who was able to reach his dream of cycling 400 miles.

☐ *Dreamers* (Yuyi Morales). This is a true story of the author's journey from her home in Xalapa, Mexico, to the U.S. with her infant son and reveals her strength, her hopes, her dreams, and her stories.

☐ *Malala:* Various versions of her story appear in picture and chapter books.

Focusing on Students' Strengths

To help learners focus on becoming resilient, we want to ensure that they become confident learners, learn to develop their skills with a sense of humor and optimism to help focus on their current strengths, and realize that their list of strengths will increase over time as they build their can dos. The activities listed in this chapter are starting points to help students on this journey. Using these activities and others like them in a classroom designed to foster resilience can provide the supports needed by many traumatized students.

For Further Study

1. **Cueing** is a tool that teachers can use to teach behaviors:

"It refers to consistently giving students a sign of some kind before starting a particular activity, preparing students to transition to this new activity. For example, a teacher may raise her hand, turn off the lights, use a short musical selection, etc., before she begins her lesson. When done consistently, it signals to students that a particular behavior (e.g., being quiet) is expected of them.

For learners who are distracted, have trouble paying attention, or who don't understand verbal instructions, cueing, when done consistently, may be particularly helpful. Cueing can become a welcome routine, and a non-verbal way to help students understand what is expected from them, since they can watch what other students do when the cue is given." (Birman, 2002, p. 40)

Create a list of cueing activities, verbal, non-verbal, including gestures and movements, with visual guidelines displayed, which would help to alleviate stress and promote learner resilience for students in your setting.

2. A grid with preventative mental health activities is presented in Table 3.1; it has been adapted from *Cultural Adjustment, Mental Health and ESL* (Adkins, Birman, & Sample, 1999, pp. 46–47). The left column includes stressors for the student. The right column contains some ideas for how to address the individual stressor. If you were to develop a workshop for your setting to help others in your school understand the issues these students face, what would you add or change to the suggested activities on the right?

TABLE **3.1**

Suggested Activities to Address Stressors

How to deal with isolation or abandonment	Activities that share interests, grouping activities that require teamwork
Loss of extended family or extended cultural community	Group or whole class discussions on hypothetical situations in which the entire group works for a solution
Moving and starting over	Field trips to interesting things in the new community
Ethnic harassment and bullying	Role playing how to deal with uncomfortable or dangerous situations, practice calling police or asking adults for help, videos of similar situations
Not understanding cultural clues	Short videos or stories that students discuss
Limited social and recreational opportunities	Field trips to community activities, map of places to go and things to do in the neighborhood

Source: Spring Institute. (1999). Used with permission.

3. "Windows and Mirrors": A recent article in *Edutopia* (Fleming, 2019) stated that children need to see story characters and stories that reflect their identities, experiences, and feelings (the mirror) plus be able to connect with and work with other cultures, customs, and beliefs (the window). How, in your own classroom, could you develop a curriculum of reading materials that address the windows and mirrors in your own classroom? What books would you choose to teach and why? How would these materials also help your students become resilient?

4. How could you use the bio cube with "I Am, I Have, I Can" writing and reflection activities with students? Describe one or more lessons for students who are at different levels of language ability. Try out these lessons and share with colleagues.

5. 100 Cameras is a non-profit organization that works with children who have had difficult or traumatic experiences (https://www.100cameras.org/model). The organization provides children with cameras to tell their stories through photography. Their curriculum includes both visual storytelling and teaching photography skills. How could you create a similar program for your students to tell their stories and recognize their journey toward resilience? How would you add written storytelling to visual storytelling?

6. Students who are interested can submit a story or artwork to the Migrant Child Storytelling website (https://migrantchildstorytelling.org). Parent approval is required. Details are available on the website and submission is free.

7. Using the checklist shown in Figure 3.5, choose picture books you want to use to build resilience and demonstrate the "power of story." Meet with a few colleagues and discuss if the books are appropriate for age/grade and language level as well as appropriate content and visuals. Consider creating your own checklist for the English learners in your setting: refugees, newcomers, SLIFE, etc. Would this checklist work? Would you add more criteria? What might you change?

FIGURE **3.5**

Checklist: Choosing Appropriate Picture Books

Picture Book Choice	Criteria	Evaluation
Is the picture book free of race, gender, and/or ethnic stereotyping?	Consider: ▪ Are photos and/or events accurate? ▪ Is culture illustrated as a caricature by representing all members as having the same features, likes, or dislikes? ▪ Does the setting include a variety of appropriate dwellings and activities for the cultural group? ▪ Are clothing, artifacts, dwellings, and activities accurate and appropriate for the cultural group?	
Are the illustrations appropriate for age/grade level? Accurate historically? Accurate representation of male/female roles in the culture?	▪ Are there age/grade appropriate children as main characters? Supporting characters? ▪ Free of cultural stereotypes and living situation? ▪ Accurately representing adult and child roles in native culture?	
Stages of adjustment and/or acculturation are shown/acknowledged.	▪ Presents a realistic portrait of English learners moving from "culture shock" to acculturation. Some stages of acculturation and adaptation are represented in text.	
Language learning is an active process.	▪ Language learning is presented in a realistic manner, through interaction and support	
Language learning is a complex process.	▪ Learning a second or new language takes time and effort, both by the student and facilitated by the teacher. Some reference to SLA and time needed.	
Learners do not abandon their primary language and culture.	▪ Learners in the text do not abandon first language and culture, so not perpetuating the idea that English is a superior language and culture.	
Additional information is presented in the narrative.	▪ Reasons for emigrating to the U.S. ▪ Self-concept (meaning of one's name) and/or identity and connections to language ▪ Fears of L1 loss ▪ Adult-child role reversal challenges	

4

Protecting Educators from the Effects of Secondary Trauma

"Caring for myself is not self-indulgence, it is self-preservation."
—Audre Lorde, *A Burst of Light*, 1988

"Teaching is one of the most rewarding jobs in the world, but it is one of the most stressful jobs as well…. Over time, unaddressed stress can negatively affect your relationships with students and your ability to support them. It is therefore critical that you stay attuned to and attend to your well-being because healthy teachers can help students flourish."
—Lee, Griffin & Keels, 2018, p. 1

The second quote comes from the introduction to Practice Brief 4 by the TREP Project (Trauma Responsive Educational Practices), which looks at the causes of job stress for educators and gives many helpful and practical suggestions for dealing with it. The report states that the key to managing stress in your life in finding a balance between the challenges of a job and how best to relax and deal with the frustrations. It explains that a person's well-being goes out of balance when the stressors exceed a person's resources to deal with the situation. Emotional and even physical health can be at risk when this occurs. The report goes on to list five key guidelines for protecting one's well-being (Lee, Griffin, & Keels, 2018):

1. Establish healthy boundaries between work and home. (This can be especially difficult for new teachers who often are already overwhelmed.)

2. Recognize and accept that you cannot meet all of your students' needs.

3. Seek and receive support if needed, both at school and out of school.

4. Establish healthy habits to protect yourself.

5. Seek and receive professional help if necessary. (p. 4)

Why Does an Educator Need Self-Care?

One of the major causes of job-related stress when working with immigrants is feeling traumatized yourself as you listen to and empathize with the situations of the students. This over-identification with the students can cause a form of trauma known as **secondary traumatic stress** or **compassion fatigue**. Many English learners come to school with traumatic backgrounds from events they experienced before arrival and often they may still be dealing with extremely stressful situations. Teachers want to help, and they feel frustrated or overwhelmed trying to fix situations, most of which are beyond their control.

An article in *Edutopia* states that "vicarious trauma affects teachers' brains in much the same way that it affects their students': The brain emits a fear response, releasing excessive cortisol and adrenaline that can increase heart rate, blood pressure, and respiration, and release a flood of emotions. This biological response can manifest in mental and physical symptoms such as anger and headaches, or workplace behaviors like missing meetings, lateness, or avoiding certain students" (Minero, 2017, p. 1).

In this same article, LeAnn Keck of Trauma Smart says that "being a teacher is a stressful enough job, but teachers are now responsible for a lot more things than just providing education.... It seems like teachers have in some ways become case workers. They get to know about their students' lives and the needs of their families, and with that can come secondary trauma" (Minero, 2017, p. 3).

This secondary trauma can be exacerbated if the teacher has a personal history of trauma or is dealing with other stressors unrelated to the students' problems. It sounds so negative to have compassion fatigue, as if a person were tired of caring. But this is the same term that is used for family members who are helping to care for ailing family members. It is not that a person stops caring, but that the act of helping can be literally draining, and the caregiver needs to take time for a refill periodically. This refill time is called **self-care**. It is "taking deliberate actions to prevent and manage experiences of stress, respect your emotional needs, nurture relationships in other areas of our life, and maintain balance between work and personal life" (Lee, Griffin, & Keels, 2018, p. 4).

There is little doubt that teaching is a stress-filled career. A study in 2005 showed that teaching is among the professions with the highest level of stress and burnout in many countries (Stoeber & Rennert, 2008). Another study (Johnson et al., 2005) showed teachers to be experiencing as much stress in their positions as paramedics and police officers. And working with students who are experiencing stress themselves only exacerbates the situation. A more recent article by a group of psychologists from the University of Missouri reported that only 7 percent of elementary teachers in their study were rated as "well-adjusted." The other 93 percent had high levels of stress and varying levels of burnout. The causes listed were the overwhelming demands of the job, managing the emotional needs of the students, and being insufficiently prepared for classroom management. They saw these stressors as causing chronic levels of exhaustion (Herman, Hickmon-Rosa, & Reinke, 2018).

So how do teachers know when they are reaching the level of burnout or compassion fatigue? There are definite warning signs of secondary trauma or compassion fatigue that an educator needs to watch for, according to *Transforming Schools: A Framework for Trauma-Engaged Practice in Alaska* (Alaska Department of Education and Early Development, 2019, p. 70):

- increased irritability or impatience with students
- difficulty planning classroom activities and lessons
- decreased concentration
- denying that traumatic events impact students
- feeling numb or detached
- intense feelings and intrusive thoughts that don't lessen over time about a student's trauma

- dreams about students' traumas
- personal involvement with a student outside the school setting

Two other possible symptoms of compassion fatigue are physical complaints similar to those experienced by children with trauma (headaches, digestion issues, exhaustion) and/or also the strong desire to escape from the people or the situation that is causing the stress (National Center on Safe Supportive Learning Environments, n.d., p. 1). For educators, this second symptom may lead to excessive absence, thoughts of inadequacy, and eventually even to the desire to leave teaching. According to a report by the National Child Traumatic Stress Network (NCTSN), "Several studies have shown that development of secondary traumatic stress often predicts that the helping professional will eventually leave the field for another type of work" (2011, p. 2).

As has become clear in this book, there is extensive research on trauma and its effects on children, but there is much less information on the effect of stress on the teacher, and also how that stress can impact a teacher's ability to be effective. One professor at the University of Virginia, Patricia Jennings, found that the "teacher's own stress level and emotional reactivity were causing problems in the classrooms" (Berdik, 2019, p. 7). So what can a teacher do to help prevent or overcome this stress?

How Can an Educator Provide Self-Care?

The best thing educators can do to protect themselves is to monitor the listed symptoms. Having some stress is definitely part of teaching, but when the level becomes overwhelming and beyond the ability to cope with typical avenues of relaxation, it is time to take a serious look at how much this stress is taking over your life. Where that line is drawn will be different for each person and may even vary in an individual's life depending on what else is occurring outside of school. It may also be affected by other stress factors at work that have little or nothing to do with the students. Whatever the reason, when the stress rises, it is time to find ways to de-stress and relax. This book focuses on helping students with a trauma background build upon their inner strengths to develop resilience. As a companion to this focus, this chapter can help the teacher find a balance between supporting our students and protecting ourselves through emotional resilience.

For each person, how to find peace and balance will vary. The National Center on Safe Supportive Learning Environments lists five areas of self-care: physical, emotional, psychological, spiritual, and professional. They also recognize that the school environment itself can be a contributor to either strengthen an educator's self-care or to add to the stress already being experienced. How a person addresses these five areas will depend upon the interests of the educator and the accessibility of each. Figure 4.1 lists some of the types of activities that could help with relaxation and restoration.

FIGURE **4.1**
Self-Care Survey

How Often Do You Do These Things?	Rarely	Sometimes	Regularly
Physical Health			
Get a full night's sleep.			
Have an adequate, healthy diet.			
Do regular exercise.			
Have regular doctor's visits.			
Take time for yourself and your family away from work.			
Emotional Health			
Find time to disconnect from work and student issues.			
See yourself and your personal and professional life realistically, knowing what you can and cannot do.			
Connect with others who can help you decompress.			
Find activities that help you relax.			
Share your frustrations with someone who can help.			
Gauge your emotional limits for helping someone else.			

Psychological Health			
Journal or blog.			
Find books or websites that give advice on self-care.			
Set limits for helping others and not allowing others to take advantage.			
Find constructive ways to support your students.			
Connect with others who can help you or your students; don't try to do everything by yourself.			
Spiritual Health			
Take time to reflect, meditate, pray, or however you are able to connect spiritually.			
Read material that helps you put life in perspective.			
Meet regularly with others who feel as you do.			
Talk to someone you trust about your feelings and frustrations.			
Professional Health			
Take some downtime every day (lunch, a small break, a snack).			
List your daily or weekly required expectations and plan how to meet them in a realistic timeframe.			
Find some peers for support and meet on a regular basis.			
Help your colleagues with their stress; don't just focus on your own.			
Leave your work at work!!			

Source: Based on the *Secondary Traumatic Stress and Self-Care Packet*, National Center on Safe Supportive Learning Environments, pp. 6–7. Used with permission.

Reflect on these activities and consider how well you are taking care of yourself to lessen or prevent the effects of secondary trauma. What are two or three things you could begin to do that would help you relax and take better care of yourself?

What Are Some of the Benefits of Self-Care?

One of the side effects of taking proper care of yourself, both physically and emotionally, is the development of **saludogens**. Just as stress can lead to the creation of pathogens causing physical illness, relaxation and decompressing can lead to positive health benefits through the release of what is known as saludogens and the Salutogenic Effect (Antonovsky, 1996).

In a workshop titled "The Importance of Stress Management and Relaxation for Emotional Wellness," Dr. Granello (2019) described how relaxation techniques and mindfulness can have definite health benefits. He explained how self-care cannot only reduce the negative effects of stress but also actually strengthen our physical and emotional defense system.

Two researchers, Mohd Khairie Ahmad and John Harrison (2007), looked at the how this Salutogenic Effect can be impacted by faith and religion. They showed how our spiritual health could impact our physical, emotional, and psychological health as well. They found that believers who followed the precepts of their faith had positive health benefits as shown in Table 4.1.

TABLE **4.1**

Religion and Health—The Salutogenic Effect

Religious Dimensions	Pathways	Mediating Factors	Salutogenic Mechanism
Religious commitment	Health-related behavior and lifestyle	Avoidance of smoking, alcohol, drug use, poor diet, unsafe sex, etc.	Lower disease risk & enhanced well-being
Involvement and fellowship	Social support and networks	Relationships with friends & family	Stress-buffering, coping and adaptation

Source: Based on work by Mohd Khairie Ahmad and John Harrison (October 16, 2007). Used with permission.

How Can a School Promote Self-Care?

Just as a welcoming and safe environment is critical for students with a trauma background, it is also necessary for the educators who serve them. Teachers and support staff need to feel that their physical, emotional, and professional lives are valued and that there are networks in place for protection and support. These support systems may be formal and part of the overall educational system, or informal and available as needed. An example of the informal type is described:

> Every Friday morning for about 15 minutes before the official start of the school day, a few teachers at an elementary school meet for a time of sharing and emotional support. Using the elements of Restorative Circles, from three to seven teachers meet each week to share concerns, decompress, and offer support to their peers. The meeting starts with a quiet time of reflection, sitting in a circle, focusing on a theme or word of the day. The teachers are asked if they want to share any specific concerns, or they may write or draw some reaction to a prompt. Each person is given time to share if desired, and a short time of quiet reflection or meditation is provided at the close. The teachers expressed their appreciation for this informal sharing time, and many stated that is helped them make it through the week.

Restorative circles are an offshoot of *restorative justice*, a term used by Howard Zehr (1990) in a book about how society needs to relook at its view of crime and punishment. He suggested bringing victims and criminals together to "restore" the community. His ideas have been carried over into school behavior plans. Usually the restorative circles in educational settings provides opportunities for students to discuss actions and reactions and to resolve behavior issues. In the situation listed, it was used for teachers to restore their professional community and find calm and strength.

There are some warning signs that indicate when a school is not the safe environment that students and staff need for security and balance. If too many of these signs (based on *The Secondary Traumatic Stress and Self-Care Packet*) are present, it may be time to address the problem at the school or even district level.

School Warning Signs That Self-Care Is Needed

Things that should alert you to the fact that self-care is needed are:

- Staff members feel unsafe or unappreciated.

- Student behavior is out of control and often requires intervention outside the classroom.

- There is a perceived lack of communication or respect between colleagues.

- Staff members lack the energy and motivation for extra projects.

- There is a high rate of staff absence or illness.

- There is a high rate of staff turnover.

The Secondary Traumatic Stress and Self-Care Packet, compiled and distributed by the National Center on Safe Supportive Learning Environments, has a number of suggestions for making schools a better place to work and teach. Teacher care cannot be seen as solely the responsibility of the educator. The workplace must provide the support needed for teachers to feel protected, supported, and valued. Some suggestions for how a school or a school district could protect its employees and keep them from the many consequences of burnout, including leaving the profession, are listed.

- The school provides all staff with professional development on stress management.

- The school or district provides an employee assistance program for additional support as needed.

- Staff members are welcome to discuss their concerns with the administration in a non-judgmental manner.

- Staff is provided regular, student-free breaks and lunches.

- There are formal, confidential channels for expressing concerns.

■ Staff satisfaction is evaluated in a confidential manner.

■ There are regular opportunities for community building for staff.

For too long, schools have been so focused on academic achievement that the social and emotional aspects of life were ignored. Most schools are becoming aware of the damage this has done to students, but they seem to be slower to realize how important it is that we provide emotional support for teachers as well. Even when a school is not as supportive as it could be, educators need to be pro-active and find ways to take care of their own professional health.

For Further Study

Choose one or more of the questions in this section as a way of focusing on yourself and self-care. Besides questions for the teacher, other questions are provided to consider what the school and the administration can do to help alleviate staff stress and compassion fatigue. Going beyond self-care, a focus group of teachers, support staff, and administrators could address what a school could do to make changes to help alleviate stress for all staff.

1. Have you ever felt the victim of compassion fatigue due to providing support for your immigrant students? What were the warning signs that you were becoming over-committed or over-stressed? How did you restore your balance?

2. Complete the Self-Care Survey (Figure 4.1), and think about two things that you could do now to help cope with stress in the classroom.

3. How well do you believe your school supports the self-care of its staff? Is there one area that you feel could be improved? How could you provide suggestions and a schoolwide plan for self-care for all educators, including paraprofessionals and support staff?

4. Were you familiar with the concept of saludogens before reading this chapter? What specifically are you doing to build saludogens in your body?

5. A book on this topic, *The Teacher Self-Care Manual: Simple Strategies for Stressed Teachers* by Patrice Palmer (2019), lists some hazards that can build stress in teachers. Are any of these hazards present in your situation or ones that you need to be more careful to avoid? What could be done to improve these situations?

   a. Classes with large numbers of students with emotional or behavioral needs that seem to drain you.

   b. Very little administrative or personal support; no one to share your frustrations or concerns.

   c. Continuous or late enrollments of students, especially true of English learners.

   d. Negative colleagues who only seem to complain and never have positive suggestions for improvement.

   e. Job situations with no benefits; having to take on multiple jobs to survive.

   f. Your own inability to say no to either (or both) students and bosses.

5

Team Response to Trauma: Beyond the Classroom

"Successful schools for English learners have a shared sense of community and responsibility."

—TESOL International Association, 2018, p. 81

A team response to support students moving from trauma to resilience in and beyond the classroom involves teachers, paraprofessionals, school personnel, families, and the community. This chapter focuses on ways that a team approach can provide maximum support for the students and help them internalize positive messages, while facing obstacles and potential negative messages. It also looks at the support personnel who work with the teacher, both in the school and beyond the school walls, to reach out to families. Additionally, the concept of the school as a reflection of acceptance and haven of safety and support for the student is reviewed.

What Does the School "Say" to the Newcomer?

The Hidden Curriculum

A personal story from one of the co-authors: Several years ago, my daughter was offered an opportunity to enroll in the middle school in which I taught. When I approached her with the possibility of moving to my school, I wasn't sure what her response would be. I thought first that she would reject this offer because she would be leaving our neighborhood school in which she had developed many friendships. To my surprise she told me, "Mom, I don't belong there. I just don't fit. I would never feel comfortable." When pressed she could not put into words what she was trying to tell me. There was, for her, a "hidden curriculum," not related to academics, but to a social-emotional climate and school culture to which she felt she did not belong.

The **hidden curriculum** is part of this subtle and possibly even subconscious school culture. "The school's culture dictates, in no uncertain terms, 'the way we do things around here.' A school's culture has far more influence on life and learning in the schoolhouse than the president of the country, the state department of education, the superintendent, the school board, or even the principal, the teachers, and parents, can ever have" (Barth, 2002, p. 6). What does this hidden curriculum project to students who are already struggling to find their place in a new environment? What can a school do to make sure that they are providing an open and welcoming aura to new arrivals of any background?

One possible solution is to bring in someone to do an impartial assessment. Jeremy Hollon works for CRIS (Community Refugee and Immigration Services), a refugee resettlement organization in Columbus, Ohio. His duties include providing support for local schools who have large numbers of refugee students. One of the services that he provides is conducting what he calls a **cultural walkthrough**, where he looks at the school through the eyes of an outsider to see how it might be perceived by families when they first arrive. He then works with the staff to help make the school more inviting, often through art. He discusses how what seems like a simple concept is actually complex: "How do you reflect the culture of a school? To me, it is working with the school and the students directly on what they want. I have to check my own artist perspective at the door and tell teachers the same thing as it isn't for us, it is for the students… From painting flags, to simple hello in a multitude of languages, to just adding color to white walls the impact can be huge. When I see students point or share with their friends at not only their language, but the work they did it can only have a positive impact on a community" (J. Hollon, personal communication, October 3, 2019).

The hidden curriculum refers to a number of unspoken, and even unwritten, behaviors and norms existing within an educational institution. Jerald noted in 2006 that the hidden curriculum "is an implicit curriculum that expresses and represents attitudes, knowledge, and behaviors, which are conveyed or communicated without aware [intention];" it is conveyed indirectly by words and actions that are part of the daily lives of everyone in a society. Loukas (2007) indicated that although it is often difficult to provide a concise definition of a school's "climate," there are three specific dimensions: physical, social, and academic.

When you enter a school, what do you see, what does the school "tell" you without words about who spends time there and how welcoming it is for a newcomer? Although educators often interpret school climate as a safe and orderly place to learn, it may not be (Jerald, 2006). But, if the focus is only on protecting instructional time from interruptions and distractions, the point of school climate is missed, he says. Additionally, "A truly positive school climate is not characterized simply by the absence of gangs, violence, or discipline problems, but also by the presence of a set of norms and values that focus everyone's attention on what is most important and motivate them to work hard toward a common purpose" (Jerald, 2006, p. 2). It is possible that the less overt types of messaging, sometimes known as micro-messaging (cues that signal that you don't belong) can be even more painful than what is more obvious.

A school's culture, or its hidden curriculum is, however, more than academics. Entering some high schools, it is obvious that the culture of the school is defined by athletic success, with showcases filled with trophies and awards, as well as banners celebrating school teams and mascots. In other schools, social popularity is celebrated with photos of social events, dances, clubs, and school plays, for example. Often there is no evidence of the work present, either artistic or written, from a diverse population of learners. There are no maps, flags, or cultural artifacts representing the diverse multicultural learners. Naturally, none of this would suggest that the school community is welcoming to the newcomer. Additionally, if all signage and examples of student success appear only in English, the hidden curriculum is quite clearly indicating that students and their families must assimilate into U.S. culture and speak only English. Therefore, everyone connected to the school—administrators, teachers, support staff, parents, and community organizations—must view the school environment for the messages newcomers and their families see when they enter the building. What does their school say without saying anything? Does it match the school's values?

Think about your school. Are changes needed to create a welcoming environment? Carefully read through the suggested criteria in Figure 5.1 for creating a welcoming environment. Consider each of the elements presented and reflect on the degree to which the element is reflected in your setting. Work with teachers, support staff, and administrators to consider what and how to implement changes.

FIGURE **5.1**

Is My School Welcoming?

Creating a Welcoming Environment	Yes, Always	Yes, Sometimes	Yes, Rarely	No, Have Not Done Before
Does the school recognize, visually or with artifacts, the multicultural population of families in the school/in the community?				
Is there a noticeable respect for diversity to anyone entering the school?				
Who welcomes visitors when they enter the school building? Is there a designated staff member or school ambassador?				
Is there visible signage directing visitors toward the front office in multiple languages?				
Does the front office staff make all newcomers feel welcome when they arrive at the school for the first time?				
Is respect for cultural diversity present when families register and complete intake documents?				
Have the intake staff, including front office, nurse, principal, and translators, as needed, been trained in how to greet and welcome new students and families?				
Have the staff and support personnel been trained in body language, facial expressions, and in visual and oral communication that would represent a visual welcoming to new families (using appropriate body language, proxemics, eye contact, slower speech, artifacts, etc.) to minimize stress and fear?				

Are bilingual community members present at intake who can help with explaining and completing documents?				
Is there a special area, room, or lounge in the school where parents can periodically meet with other parents and school staff? Is a translator available?				
Has the school worked to ensure the school is safe for all learners? Is the physical environment well-maintained, well-monitored by staff, well-lit, and chaos-free?				
Are rules and regulations posted in multiple languages and shared with immigrant families upon intake and available for parent meetings? Are these documents available throughout the year to review rules, as well as to help field questions and concerns?				
Are school manuals/school policies created with pictures and captions in multiple languages to help newcomers and families understand key information?				
Does the school encourage students to participate in all school activities—from sports, to the arts, to clubs, etc.? How do can you tell? Is there information about how to join the band, chorus, art club, drama club, teams, etc., in signage in English and other languages in the school?				

Other Ways to Create a Welcoming Atmosphere

Produce a Culturally Accessible School Handbook

School handbooks or school manuals should be available and contain vital information about school procedures, start and end times of the school day, where and when transportation is available, school dress codes, required school supplies, what to do if you child is not well, and many other topics. The handbook should be translated into students' native languages by proficient speakers of that language; in addition, proficient speakers of the language could also assist with the development of teacher resource information to provide insights into the culture. If no written translation for the handbook is possible (e.g., unusual dialect, no written language, and/or no native language speaker available), a picture version of the school handbook with single words or short phrases can be developed. Some schools create video versions with spoken instructions in the native language for populations with limited literacy. One example of an accessible handbook can be found from Redmond, Oregon: http://redmond.k12.or.us/files/2014/01/Newcomers-Visual-Daily-Schedule-Example.docx.

At the very least, all school manuals should include:

- a color-coded school calendar, including half-day schedules, vacation, professional development days for staff, etc.

- information about the start and end of the school day

- directions regarding where to drop off and pick up learners before and after school

- directions to the main office, nurse's office, gym, media center, etc., and how to and when to connect with each of these key personnel

- visual models of emergency card information, as well as any other intake documents

- an infographic to represent procedures to follow if the child is ill

- what is required for school supplies and school uniforms (if relevant), including clothing required for physical education

- playground and lunchroom procedures

Develop a Trauma-Informed Staff

Supporting the emotional safety for students who have experienced trauma requires that the staff be trained by school counselors and/or social workers about the importance of providing a respectful, calm environment. Additionally, as discussed in Chapter 2, it is important to review and prepare and/or explain to students and families about trauma-potential triggers, such as fire drills and other large group events that have crowds or noise (e.g., moving between classes and the school bell system), which could cause a traumatic response or flashback. Social workers, counselors, and outside community personnel who are trained in trauma response can help prepare all teachers become aware of triggers of other potentially traumatic incidents, such as bullying, bias, unresolved conflict, and incidents of disrespect. It's essential that all school personnel learn how to approach and resolve these types of incidents, how to lower the stress level throughout the school, and to know when to and how to request additional and/or outside help.

Setting aside specific classrooms other school locations to provide a no-stress or quiet area for students and to sit, reflect, draw, read, listen to calming sounds, or meditate (see Think–Wait–Respond in Chapter 3) is good practice. In addition to encouraging moments to de-stress when students return to group and/or class activities, these spaces can help set behavioral expectations that are clear and enforced consistently. For example, other school locations require specific behaviors—gyms allow for activity and non-quiet time and libraries allow for quiet and study. (A good time to introduce behavioral expectations would be during the morning meeting; see Chapter 3.)

We believe that, although this may be a difficult challenge at times because of the language and the cultural barriers that exist on both sides of the school door, the benefits are definitely worth the effort.

Develop a Professional Support Staff

Another vital piece to providing the assistance is professional support from counselors and trained therapists. For some students, their lives have been so shattered that they require the intervention of mental health specialists. However, one of the difficulties in providing this support for immigrant students is the stigma attached to mental health services in many cultures.

And even for the families who are willing and even eager to receive this help, finances and transportation may prevent access.

One way that many schools have been able to overcome these types of barriers is through school-based mental health clinics. When parents see the clinic personnel as school employees (even though they may not be), they are often more willing to allow their children to access the help. Bilingual personnel are more accessible as translators and can communicate with parents about transportation to/from meetings and other issues. And, in many cases, the clinics are run through grants or as outreach clinics of more established programs, so the costs are either extremely reasonable or even free.

In fact, one study reported that parents were twice as likely to access these services when they were located inside the school building, that the children showed positive changes in behavior at home, and that the students made more academic progress in school-based clinics than separate off-site programs (Atkins et al., 2006). Furthermore, because U.S. schools expect parental involvement, they are ideally suited to serving as an avenue to engage parents in interventions and to help create a bridge between the worlds of family and school in ways that do not stigmatize the family or the child.

Developing Home-School Connections

Home Visits: "Our Beloved Community"

The 2019 SIOP National Conference plenary talked about Dr. Martin Luther King, Jr.'s vision for a better America, what he called "our beloved community." The speaker (Short, 2019) stated that a welcoming atmosphere was present throughout certain schools she had visited and encouraged an inclusive vision that not only advocates for academics, but also "respects, affirms, and promotes students' home languages and cultural knowledge and experiences, as resources." Creating this type of welcoming atmosphere and supporting families includes parent liaison and/or social workers, as well as interpreters who are on call as needed. Schools should provide translation of essential home/school communication and connections to community social services.

Reaching out and supporting families through home visits that are strategically organized to initiate communication and welcome families to their new community is critical. Included in the planning should be essential school and community information that is shared by staff, not only about the curriculum but also school and community services, including initial health screenings offered by school nurses. Home visits should consist of teams, including a native-language speaker who is a paraprofessional. In each home visit, the message should be clear that the school respects and encourages the maintenance of home language as important for the family and its culture.

The home visit team needs to also listen to the family. Newcomer families come with hopes, dreams, wishes, and concerns for the health and safety of their children. Immigrant families want a better life for their children; they want them to read more, become better at math, and put more effort into their studies. Home visits can help families find ways to ensure that these goals can be met.

Common Misconceptions about Immigrant Families

Unfortunately, misconceptions abound about immigrant families when there is little communication, as noted in "Why Are We Still Blaming the Families in 2019?" (Peralta, 2019). This editorial discussed what school visit teams learned that surprised them: For example, families spent a significant amount of time making sure their children complete their assignments. In another instance, contrary to teacher beliefs, when one family would return to Mexico for their annual two- to three-month trip, the school assumed it was a "vacation." However, it was discovered that this return trip was to help the grandparents and other family members, as well as to maintain cultural and linguistic ties to family. Finally, with this knowledge, garnered from home visits, school teams had a deeper understanding of students' home lives and cultures, and could build on this with culturally relevant texts that would engage students and build classroom community.

Resources for Reaching Out to Families

There are several excellent resources available for schools who are looking for additional methods to connect with families and increase community ties.

1. *Educational Leadership's* September 2017 themed issue is entitled "In Sync with Families" and provides several articles with ideas for connecting with immigrant and English learner families in school, for school events, and through home visits.

2. *Language Arts: A National Council of Teachers of English Journal* (Lee, Hoekje, & Levine, 2018) describes a program called Project LIFE (Literacy for Immigrant Family Engagement) in "Introducing Technology to Immigrant Families to Support Early Literary Development and Two-Generation Learning." The Project LIFE's seven workshops focused on modeling specific early literacy strategies. Parents learn the strategies in the workshops and then practice them at home with their children. Some topics included how to use questioning strategies with the child to promote discussion and how to interact with the child around writing. Parents were also introduced to a variety of online resources, including video texts in Spanish and storytelling e-books in multiple languages.

3. Another resource, providing a comprehensive approach to building partnerships with families, is a model developed by SEDL (Southwest Educational Development Laboratory) and the U.S. Department of Education entitled *Partners in Education: A Dual Capacity-Building Framework for Family-School Partnerships*. The dual-capacity building framework, provided in an **infographic**, is a model for supporting effective home-school partnerships (Mapp & Kuttner, 2013, p. 8). It guides schools systematically through the process, demonstrating how to move from focusing on the challenges to: articulating the initiative and interventions; creating the conditions for success in a family school partnership; identifying the intermediate goals focusing on family engagement policies and programs not only at the local level, but also at the state and federal levels; and focusing on capacity-building outcomes for the school, program staff, and families.

When following this framework, it is important to note that the framework should be implemented with fidelity and consistency to ensure that learners are supported as they move from trauma to resilience. When implemented effectively, schools are able to form lasting relationships among the family, the home culture, and the school. Staff and family partnership have outcomes that would promote student language development, leadership, and achievement, including:

- recognizing and honoring immigrant families' knowledge, skills, and cultures.
- sustaining a school culture that is welcoming to families and promotes family engagement.
- connecting family engagement to student language development and learning.
- valuing family as decision-makers of educational options for their children.

An effective partnership with families can only be achieved if there is a clear plan and set of guidelines to develop school goals that respect and support languages and cultures, and also support student learning and social-emotional development resources for all staff.

4. The Office of English Language Acquisition working with the U.S. Department of Education has prepared a *Newcomer Tool Kit* (U.S. Department of Education, 2016) that is available online that will prepare staff to better understand newcomers and their needs. Prepare staff for home visits to understand the needs of newcomers and their families. The Newcomer Tool Kit (see Chapter 1) provides information about newcomers from a profile of this diverse population through high-quality instruction to meet newcomer social and emotional needs, including partnerships with families. Reviewing key information before making home visits and keying in on the specific needs of the family teams are to visit is vital to the success of a home visit.

How Can Paraprofessionals Support English Learners with Trauma?

Working with Teachers and Parents

The role of the paraprofessional in a L2 classroom cannot be overemphasized. They often serve as a critical bridge between the home and the school.

In Birman's discussion of what schools can do to support immigrants with trauma, she emphasizes that what is needed most is a "range of strategies that teacher, as well as the paraprofessional, can use to enhance the child's academic and behavioral functioning regardless of diagnosis" (Birman et al., 2007, p. 15). It is often the paraprofessional who has the time and the small group opportunities to provide supports that the mainstream and even the ESL or bilingual teacher cannot.

Connecting to *The 6 Principles*

Chapter 2 discussed *The 6 Principles for Exemplary Teaching of English Learners*® (TESOL, 2018) in reference to the teacher. Here we focus on the important role of the paraprofessional in supporting learners as they move from trauma to resilience because Principle 1 (Know Your Learners) applies to paraprofessionals as well. Paraprofessionals often work directly with students for a significant part of each school day, so they must know as much about the student as possible.

Paraprofessionals should be included in all emails, meetings, and intake for each newly arrived student. They are the liaison with families upon arrival by providing information in students' native language regarding how school "works," schedules, needed school materials, daily school schedules, etc. They are a resource for parents and help to encourage families to share information about the child's experience before arriving. They can translate and/or interpret information for parents, including meetings, conferences, and notes home, and can make phone calls when needed. Paraprofessionals overall can ease the transition into school life for families and students.

On a social-emotional learning level, paraprofessionals can share their own stories with students, especially if they themselves, or members of their families, have been English learners. Sharing one's own experiences related to arriving in a new country, learning the language, both struggling and succeeding, can help to ease the stress of newcomers and to motivate them.

Paraprofessionals play an important role in carrying out Principle 2 (Create Conditions for Language Learning) because they can help students feel at ease in a classroom culture that is both safe and welcoming. Specifically, paraprofessionals can:

- Assist the teacher by helping to create a welcoming and organized classroom, which includes:
  - ☐ starting each day with an atmosphere that welcomes each new student for the first few weeks.
  - ☐ helping students learn classroom routines, comprehend schedules, and understand expected classroom behavior and instructional activities.
  - ☐ providing access to native language resources when possible.

- Focus on language that values the students and their learning, which includes:
  - ☐ praising efforts and accomplishments with supportive language, both in English and students' native language, when possible.
  - ☐ praising students when using native language to understand new learning.
  - ☐ helping students to understand how translanguaging can help them to strategically make meaning of new learning.
  - ☐ setting high expectations, encouraging students to take risks in learning, and praising their efforts, with the teacher.
  - ☐ keeping students engaged and motivated through guidance and support.

Building Supportive Relationships through Activities

Paraprofessionals can help learners build their resilience in non-academic ways. They can build supportive relationships with students, promote positive peer relationships, and model kindness and respect for all learners. They can help students exposed to trauma and adversity learn how to use mindful activities to deal with a variety of difficult feelings (Stewart, 2017).

Since the paraprofessional spends more one-on-one time with learners, the activities can be practiced in an area where the learner feels safe. A few examples of these are:

- *Safekeeping:* Ask students to write or draw what is bothering or worrying them on a sheet of paper. Newcomers determine if they wish to share it or not. Then they take the paper and place it in a box. Later, they can read the worry and determine if they can discard or keep it for a little more time.

- *The Inner Me:* The student and a partner each create a picture of themselves that show how they look and how they feel. Then they create picture of their partner. Together the students compare all four pictures and describe what they see and how they feel. Discuss how they see themselves and how their partner sees them. Older students can write a few words, phrases or sentences. The paraprofessional can help students think positively about who they are now and how others see them.

- *I Am Thankful:* Near the end of the school day, students are asked to think about a person or thing they like or something great that happened to them. Then they draw a picture or write about what it is. They take it home and keep the message or the drawing beside their bed and look at it before going to sleep and when they wake up. They try to remember the good things that are happening in their life.

- *Loving Kindness:* Students are asked to sit in a chair and hold their hand over their heart and state: " May I be happy. May I be safe. May I be peaceful. May I be kind." They repeat the same sentences for a friend or family member and then for someone they do not know.

- *Everything Changes:* Students observe changes around them. These observations can include noticing weather changes, plants, physical growth, a new student who joins the ESL class, or how their feelings change during the school day. Newcomers can write, draw, or talk about the changes they notice and how they make them feel. Create a positive focus on now and in the future through expressing an understanding that everything changes.

Providing Emotional Support: A Three-Tier Interventional Approach

In *Trauma-Sensitive Schools for the Adolescent Years,* Susan E. Craig (2017) discusses a three-tiered system of trauma support, using a public health model, implemented in three tiers, and determined by the needs for student academic support. She indicates that the benefits of differentiated instruction, in a system of tiered interventions, would go beyond academics to include helping "teens in their developing a sense of self-efficacy and self-awareness" (p. 4). Her tier system mirrors that of the traditional RTI (Response to Intervention) three tiers used in K–12 settings, and would be implemented with both trained educators and paraprofessionals as follows for at-risk learners at all grades:

- *Tier I:* Developmentally appropriate instruction for all students is implemented in the general education classroom with paraprofessional support. Appropriate pacing, materials, assignments, and assessments that address the differentiated needs of all students are incorporated in instruction. Teacher notes and running records follow students' progress both for academic and SEL. The teacher meets with other teachers, including specific paraprofessionals who provide classroom support and shares notes, assessments, and observations.

- *Tier II:* Multiple and varied supports needed for instruction and SEL would be provided by an instructional specialist in a small-group setting, along with the support of native-language paraprofessional (when possible) and SEL specialists as needed.

- *Tier III:* More frequent interventions are instituted; often one-on-one or in groups of no more than two or three. Targeted academic needs and specific SEL issues are addressed. School psychologists and/or social workers are involved in addressing these concerns. Academic specialists target the learning needs, along with one-on-one support from paraprofessionals.

Based on our experiences with English learners, we believe that a non-traditional, more fluid approach is appropriate: Begin with small group instruction (Tier III) for students with the most severe trauma issues and especially for those with beginning-level English skills and interrupted academic backgrounds. This intensive intervention would be the ideal opportunity to introduce both social and academic English especially to new arrivals in a safe, small group, focused on their specific needs. As the students feel comfortable and are more able to work in a larger group setting, move from Tier III to Tier II, creating additional opportunities for increased oral and written interaction, including improving social-emotional self-confidence. In both of these tiers, the majority of the school day would continue to be with their peers, with portions of the day held in small group settings.

When students have progressed through the Tier III and II, they can move comfortably to a whole group setting for the entire day. Finally, students can move to Tier I, continuing to use Tier II or even Tier III for gaps in SEL requiring a small group approach. Paraprofessionals who have been trained in social-emotional supports can lead much of the Tier III small group activity under the supervision and guidance of trained teachers and counselors.

Final Thoughts

We close by recommending ways that a school can encourage supportive relationships, including collaborating with local immigrant communities, educating parents in their expected role in Western schools, and engaging parents in school events as much as possible, based on Morland et al. (2013).

Figure 5.2 lists the type of risks most immigrant and refugee children have experienced, what strengths they needed for survival, and what schools can do to build upon these strengths to enable students to continue on their journey to resilience. We have added one column to the grid (What I Can Do) so readers have space to consider a specific action they want to take in your own setting. What can you share with others who are facing similar situations?

FIGURE **5.2**

Immigrant Children: Promoting Resilience in School

Risks and Challenges	Student Strengths	Suggestions for Promoting Resilience in School	What Specifically I Can Do in My Setting
Traumatic migration journeys	Successfully overcoming migration stress and transitioning to a new country can increase sense of self-efficacy, self-confidence, and autonomy.	Establish safety and predictability in the classroom. Share stories (within limits of comfort, in supportive context). Focus on strengths and successes.	
Separation from immediate and extended family members, loss of friends, community support	Supportive relationships with adults and peers. School belonging and connectedness.	Build sense of community in classroom. Use mentoring programs. Engage ethnic community leaders in school activities.	
Resettlement stress	Cohesive family and co-ethnic community. Language and cultural services of local school. Limited language brokering for family.	Know community service systems for immigrants. Work with school social workers, psychologists, and counselors to ensure that the entire family is linked with services that will benefit the child's learning.	
Language and cultural differences and transitions; acculturation stress	Cognitive flexibility and problem-solving skills. Language and cultural competency skills that increase sense of self-efficacy. Conflict-resolution skills.	Ensure accurate assessment. Support maintaining both languages and biculturalism. Engage families in school.	
Low-literacy, limited, or interrupted formal education	Highly value education as path to success. Sacrifice by parents and students to prioritize school.	Use transitional programs such as ESL, newcomer programs, and family literacy.	
Discrimination due to race, religion, language, or other difference	Ethnic pride. Grounding in family, culture, religion, and larger sense of purpose.	Teach and celebrate difference. Promote tolerance and social justice. Promote positive school climate.	

For Further Study

Choose one or more of the questions that would be most relevant for your setting. Work alone or with other teachers and paraprofessionals in your setting to explore key topics in this chapter that will help make changes and improvements to meet the needs of all stakeholders.

1. Consider the benefits to demystifying the hidden curriculum, including increasing student motivation, improving school and class climate, improving student confidence and perseverance, decreasing emotional stress, and creating a community of learners. Create a table or chart that defines why this happens and provide an example of an activity or procedure that would exemplify this benefit of demystifying the hidden curriculum. Share your list with colleagues.

2. Design your own infographic or flowchart developing your school/district plan for a dual capacity-building framework for your own family-school partnerships. How would you determine your needs based on your population (e.g., refugees, immigrants, newcomers, etc.)? How could you change your needs into actions? How would you help all partners learn about the diverse cultures and languages in your setting? What would it look like?

3. Take a critical look at the current school handbook used in your building. Assemble a team to develop a more parent-friendly version of the handbook with additional visuals. Who could you include in this endeavor? How could you determine its effectiveness in conveying important information?

4. Form a study group of teachers, paraprofessionals, and support staff such as media specialists, school nurses, and/or guidance counselors to look at Figure 5.2. Consider what each person in your study group could do to complete the final column of the grid. Create a chart of specific ideas generated and share with all staff.

Appendix
Personal Migration and/or Resilience Narratives

These resources can be used for academic, SEL, and/or self-study for educators. The first list of picture books contains stories that narrate the personal stories of children who have faced difficult situations, been forced to leave their homes, or overcome adversity; the second list is for examining mindfulness. The chapter books provide a more in-depth narrative of this journey, while the games include suggested activities. Note that some books appear in multiple categories.

Picture Books about Migration and/or Resilience

Abouraya, K. L. (2014). **Malala Yousafzai: Warrior with Words**. Star-Walk KidsMedia. The story of Malala's bravery.

Arqueta, J. (2016). **Somos como los nubos: We Are Like the Clouds.** Groundwood Books. A book of poetry about the dangerous journey from El Salvador to the U.S.

Aweng, B. B. (2018). **The Journey of Hope.** Bolaweng.com. The story of one of the Lost Boys of Sudan.

Bunting, E. (2006). **One Green Apple**. Clarion Books. Farah, a newcomer, feels all alone even when she is on a field trip with her classmates.

Clinton, C. (2017). **She Persisted: 13 American Women Who Changed the World.** Philomel Books. Stories of American women in history who changed the U.S. and the world with their persistence.

Curtis, J. L., & Cornell, L. (2016). **This Is Me.** Workman Publishing. A book about leaving home and starting over in a new country.

Essa, H. (2016). **Teach Us Your Name.** A book about the importance of using a child's real name and pronouncing it accurately.

Garza, C. L. (1990). **Family Pictures/Cuadros de Familia.** Children's Book Press. A bilingual picture book about a child's memories of Mexico.

Giovanni, N. (2005). **Rosa.** Henry Holt and Co. The story of Rosa Parks who boycotted segregation on public buses. This a Caldecott Honor Book.

Hoffman, M. (1992). **The Colour of Home.** Francis Lincoln Children's Books. The story of a young Somali boy who is helped through his adjustment to school by a teacher.

Hyman, T. S. (1983). **Tight Times.** Puffin Books. Poverty impacts a young boy's life.

King, D. (2010). **I See the Sun in Nepal.** Satya House. A girl remembers her life in Nepal.

Kittinger, J. S. (2010). **Rosa's Bus: The Ride to Civil Rights**. Calkins Creek Press. The story of the bus ride with lots of background on Rosa Parks' life.

Kuntz, D., & Shrodes, A. (2017). **Lost and Found Cat: The True Story of Kunkush's Incredible Journey.** Random House. The story of a cat that is lost and later found as an Iraqi family makes a dangerous ocean crossing into Greece.

Lord, M. (2008). **A Song for Cambodia**. Lee and Low. The true story of a boy who survives the Khmer Rouge through his music.

McGill, D. (2018). **I Won't Quit: A Teaching Perseverance Book**. Trendwood Press. Cady faces a series of obstacles in her life but perseveres.

Moore-Mallinos, J. (2005). **Do You Have a Secret?** Barron's Education. Secrets can be fun; however, some secrets can hurt you. Helping children know what to do when they have a problem.

Munsch, R., & Saoussan, A. (1995). **From Far Away**. Annick Press Ltd. Story of a family, told by the daughter, fleeing their country when war starts in their city. They come to North America from "far away."

Perez, A. I. (2009). **My Diary from Here to There/Mi Diario de Aqui Hasta Alla.** Children's Book Press. A bilingual book about a girl's journey from Mexico to California. Pura Belpré Award for Writing.

Reynolds, P. H. (2018). **The Word Collector**. Orchard Books. A young boy discovers the power of the words all around him.

Silver, G. (2009). **Anh's Anger.** Plum Blossom Books. A Vietnamese boy's journey to overcome his anger.

Sornson, B. (2013). **Stand in My Shoes: Kids Learning about Empathy.** Love & Logic Press. After Emily asks her big sister what the word *empathy* means, Emily decides to pay closer attention to others during her day.

Spilsbury, L.

- (2016). **Children in Our World: Global Conflict.** Barron's. A non-fiction book that explains how global conflicts occur and their impact.

- (2016). **Refugees and Migrants: Global Conflict.** Barron's. A non-fiction book that explains who refugees and migrants are and why they are forced to flee.

Uchida, Y. (1993). **The Bracelet.** Penguin Young Readers Group. Introduces the WWII internment experience told through the eyes of a young Japanese girl in California.

Van Wyk, C. (2009) **Nelson Mandela: Long Walk to Freedom.** Macmillan Children's Books. Picture book version of Mandela's official autobiography of the same name.

Williams, M. (2005). **Brothers in Hope.** Lee and Low. The story of the Lost Boys of Sudan.

Winter, J. (2009). **Nasreen's Secret School: A True Story from Afghanistan.** Simon and Schuster. The story of a girl's school in Afghanistan under the Taliban.

Yousafzai, M. (2017). **Malala's Magic Pencil.** Little, Brown, and Co. Malala wished for a magic pencil to draw a lock on her door to keep her brothers out of her room.

Picture Books for Mindfulness and/or Resilience

Clinton, C. (2017) **She Persisted around the World: 13 Women Who Changed History.** Philomel Books. Biographies of women who rose up, broke barriers, and shaped history.

Garcia, G.

- (2017). **Listening with My Heart: A Story of Kindness and Self-Compassion.** Skinned Knee Publishing. The book focuses on how to help a child develop a natural capacity for empathy, kindness, and self-compassion.

- (2018). **I Can Do Hard Things: Mindful Affirmations for Kids**. Skinned Knee Publishing. Teaching affirmation about dealing with difficult situations.

Hazen, B. S. (1983). **Tight Times.** Penguin Putnam Books for Young Readers. A family going through difficult financial times.

Holmes, M. M. (2000). **A Terrible Thing Happened**. Magination Press/American Psychological Association. About a child who has experienced a traumatic event and who is at first unable to talk about the experience with an adult. The afterword for parents provides suggestions and resources to help traumatized children.

Jimenez, F. (1998*)*. **La Mariposa.** Houghton Mifflin. A picture book companion to *The Circuit*. Helps children understand transformation through the story of butterflies. Includes a Spanish word/phrase glossary. It symbolically follows the child's observations of the caterpillar becoming a butterfly, while mirroring Jimenez's story of his struggles to learn English and achieve his goal of going to college.

Kroll, V. (2005). **Equal Shmequal.** Charlesbridge. What is the meaning of equal? Through a story revolving around animals and a tug-of-war, the reader discovers what equal means for each of us.

McGill, D. (2018). **I Won't Quit: A Teaching Perseverance Book.** Trendwood Press. Cady faces a series of obstacles in her life, but she is able to persevere.

O'Brien, A. S. (2015). **I'm New Here.** Charlesbridge. Primary-level book about being the new child in the classroom.

Reynolds, P.H.

- (2003). **The Dot.** Candlewick Press. The story how even an "angry" dot can be a symbol of self-expression in drawing.
- (2004). **Ish.** Candlewick Press. A young boy is upset with the quality of his drawings until his sister points out their special quality.
- (2019). **Say Something.** Orchard Books. A child's voice can heal, transform, or change the world.

Sotomayor, S. (2019). **Just Ask: Be Different, Be Brave, Be You.** Philomel Books. Told by the U.S. Supreme Court justice, a narrative of how children can use their strengths to work together and learn about each other.

Wright, L.

- (2016). **Mindful Mantras: I Can Handle It!** Helps students handle tough situations through self-talk.
- (2019). **Mindful Mantras: I Can Handle It 2!** Helps children handle anxious and overwhelming feelings.
- (2018). **Mindful Mantras: I Will Be Okay!** Helps young learners understand their fears and concerns and understand they will be okay.

Yamasaki, K. (2013). **Fish for Jimmy.** Houghton House Books. One brother is determined to help his sibling by fishing to make sure that they both have familiar food to eat.

Games for Mindfulness

Sargent, K. (2020). **Mindful Games for Kids: 50 Fun Activities to Stay Present, Improve Concentration, and Understand Emotions.** Rockridge Press. (Ages 4–8)

Stewart, W. (2017). **Mindful Kids: 50 Mindfulness Activities for Kindness, Focus, and Calm.**

Chapter Books about Migration and/or Resilience

Alabed, B. (2017). **Dear World: A Syrian Girl's Story of War and Plea for Peace.** Simon and Schuster. The true story of a young girl who tweets about the war in Syria as she experiences it.

Applegate, K. (2007). **Home of the Brave.** Macmillan. The story of a resettled refugee boy from South Sudan.

Asgedom, M. (2004). **Of Beetles and Angels: A Boy's Remarkable Journey from a Refugee Camp to Harvard.** Mawi, Inc. An autobiographical account of a family from Ethiopia that relocates to Chicago as refugees.

Barakat, I. (2007). **Tasting the Sky: A Palestinian Childhood**. Farrar, Straus, and Giroux. A memoir of a young girl's life in Palestine that included war, occupation, separation, and resilience.

Beah, I. (2007). **A Long Way Gone: Memoirs of a Boy Soldier.** Farrar, Straus, and Giroux. The true story of a teen who was forced into a paramilitary group in Sierra Leone and his eventual escape and rehabilitation.

Colfer, O., & Donkin, A. (2018). **Illegal**. Sourcebooks. A graphic novel about a boy who escapes Africa on a boat headed to Europe and the difficulties he faces.

Gratz, A. (2017). **Refugee**. Scholastic Press. The intertwining of three refugee boys over time, from Nazi Germany, Castro's Cuba, and in modern-day Syria.

Guerrero, D. (2018). **My Family Divided: One Girl's Journey of Home, Loss, and Hope.** Henry, Holt & Co. True story of Diane's family torn apart by deportation. Diane is an actor who stars in *Orange Is the New Black* TV show.

Jiminez, F. (1997). **The Circuit: Stories from the Life of a Migrant Child.** University of New Mexico Press. Autobiography of Francisco Jiminez's life as the son of a migrant worker. This is the first of four autobiographical books beginning with childhood and ending as a professor at Santa Clara University.

Lai, T. (2011). **Inside Out and Back Again.** Harper Collins. A story of a girl during the Vietnam War.

Mead, A. (2003). **Year of No Rain.** Farrar, Straus, and Giroux. A fictionalized account of the story of the Lost Boys of Sudan.

Naidoo, B. (2004). **Making It Home.** International Rescue Committee. A series of stories about refugee children.

Nazario, S. (2014). **Enrique's Journey: The True Story of a Boy Determined to Reunite with his Mother (The Young Adult Adaptation).** Ember Books. Description of the journey many Central American teens make to come to the U.S. A journalist undertakes the typical trip that Central American migrants take to reach the U.S./Mexico border. There are two versions of this narrative: one for adolescents and one for adults.

Neumann, R. (ed). (2018). **I Am Home: Portraits of Immigrant Teenagers.** Parallax Press. Vignettes of students from an international high school in California.

Park, L. S. (2010). **A Long Walk to Water.** Houghton Mifflin Harcourt. A story about the Lost Boys of Sudan told through the eyes of the experiences of one boy walking to safety. Based on a true story, the author weaves two separate stories from the Sudan, about a girl in 2008 and a boy in 1985 (one of the Lost Boys) around the theme of the hardships both encounter and how water symbolizes this theme.

Pinkney, A. D. (2014). **The Red Pencil.** Little, Brown, and Company. A story about a girl in a Darfur refugee camp.

Tonatiah, D. (2018). **Undocumented: A Worker's Fight.** Harry N. Abrams. Story of issues facing undocumented workers from Mexico.

Vargas, J. A. (2018). **Dear America: Notes of an Undocumented Citizen.** Dey Street Books. True story of a Filipino youth who discovered he was not in the U.S. legally when he applied for college. He is a Pulitzer Prize–winning journalist.

Yousafzai, M. (2016). **I Am Malala: How One Girl Stood Up for Education and Changed the World** (Young Readers Ed.). Little, Brown Books. Autobiographical account of a girl from Pakistan who was shot by the Taliban for attending school.

Professional Resources on Trauma and/or Resilience

Brock, A., & Hundley, H. (2016). **The Growth Mindset Coach: A Teacher's Month-by-Month Handbook for Empowering Students to Achieve**. Ulysses Press. This book, organized around the academic calendar from August to July, offers one topic per month for teachers to read, reflect upon, and then utilize in their classrooms. Great for a book-study group.

Craig, S. (2017). **Trauma-Sensitive Schools for the Adolescent Years: Promoting Resiliency and Healing, Grades 6-12**. Teacher's College Press. With a focus on teenagers, this book looks specifically at how trauma impacts middle and high school students. Each chapter gives specific suggestions for both teachers and administrators.

Flaitz, J. (2018). **Refugee Students: What Every Teacher Needs to Know**. University of Michigan Press. A handy guide to the basics of refugees, including who they are and what teachers can do to support them.

Hammond, Z. (2015). **Culturally Responsive Teaching and the Brain**. Corwin Press. This book is a blend of two major hot topics in education, showing teachers how to adapt their lessons to best meet the linguistic and cultural backgrounds of their students.

Medley, R. M. (2017). **Resilience: Bouncing Back through English**. Westbow Press. A book of lesson plans to help build resilience for the adolescent or adult classroom.

Morland, L., & Birman, D. (2020). A chapter on immigrant students in **Supporting and Educating Traumatized Students (2ⁿᵈ Ed.)**. Oxford University Press. This is a revision of a 2013 chapter. It lists many of the challenges that immigrant children face in education and offers many practical suggestions for supporting them.

Romero, V., Robertson, R., & Warner, A. (2018). **Building Resilience in Students Impacted by Adverse Childhood Experiences: A Whole-Staff Approach**. Corwin Press. Combining information with staff development activities, this book could be used for school-wide trainings.

Shapiro, S., Farrelly, R., & Curry, M.J. (Eds.). (2018). **Educating Refugee-Background Students: Critical Issues and Dynamic Contexts.** Multilingual Matters. An edited correction of empirical studies on refugee education around the world.

Sorrels, B. (2015). **Reaching and Teaching Children Exposed to Trauma**. Gryphon House. Practical tools and strategies for teachers and care-givers to help young learners heal.

Souers, K. (with Hall, P.) (2016). **Fostering Resilient Learners: Strategies for Creating a Trauma-Sensitive Classroom**. ASCD. The authors explore childhood trauma and its impact on motivation, learning, and teaching. Each chapter focuses on reflection.

Van Der Kolk, B. (2014). **The Body Keeps the Score: Brain, Mind, and Body in the Healing of Trauma.** Penguin Books. The author uses his own research and that of other specialists to present a comprehensive approach to how the power of relationships can help to heal.

Wink, J. (2018). **The Power of Story**. Libraries Unlimited. The author's goal is to help readers use storytelling in their personal and professional lives to facilitate explaining and expanding on complex concepts and experiences.

Zacarian, D., Alvarez-Ortiz, L., & Haynes, J. (2017). **Teaching to Strengths: Supporting Students Living with Trauma, Violence, and Chronic Stress**. ASCD. As the title implies, focusing on what students can do is the basis for building resilience.

Glossary

ACEs (adverse childhood experiences)—a series of questions that were used in a study by the CDC and Kaiser Permanente in 1995–1997, in which they looked at how childhood experiences affected adult health and behaviors. The surprising links they found have impacted how doctors look at both physical and mental health in children and adults.

acculturation—the process of a person learning to adapt to a new situation. It focuses on choosing when, where, and how much to blend in. Acculturation is in contrast to assimilation, which subsumes the previous life in favor of the new one.

acute stressor—a situation or event that causes extreme fear or frustration. It is short in duration but intense.

asylee/asylum-seeker—Asylees, or asylum-seekers, are a separate category of immigrant. They are individuals who enter the United States and then ask for official permission to stay. They must prove a well-founded fear of persecution the same as a refugee, but the difference is that they ask after they enter the U.S., not before. The U.S. government does not consider asylees as refugees until and unless their case is approved.

bio cube—a paper cube on which information is written about a person's life in sections or categories. Bio cubes can focus on one biographical event or the writer's entire life.

calming center—an area in a classroom where students can have an opportunity to de-escalate negative behavior. The location is separate from the main teaching/learning area in the classroom. In comfortable seating, a learner is offered time and space to refocus with non-academic resources available, such as coloring or drawing materials, squishy balls to squeeze, or calming music to listen to. Journal writing is encouraged and shared with the teacher in order for the student to express what triggered the response.

chronic stress—stress that occurs over an extended period of time and can have negative effects on both physical and mental health.

chronic stressor—a situation or event that occurs over a sustained period of time. It can be of less intensity than an acute stressor, but it lasts longer.

collage—a work of art that contains multiple smaller pieces, often from various types of material or media.

compassion fatigue—a term that defines how a person can feel who is working with others who are experiencing trauma. Signs of compassion fatigue can be withdrawal from interaction with others, frustration, or anger.

complex trauma—trauma that is the result of long-term exposure to stress, including several interconnected stressors.

cueing—involves a teacher giving a certain sign that indicates that some activity or change is coming—for example, that it is time to line up for lunch.

cultural walkthrough—looking at a school or other location to determine how well diversity is represented.

dialogue journal—students write in a journal on a set schedule either as freewriting/reflecting or on a teacher-initiated topic. The journal is then shared with a writing partner or the teacher, who responds to the contents of the entry with comments, questions, or additional reflections.

empathy—being able to feel compassion and understanding toward another person.

grit—not giving up; staying strong against adverse conditions.

growth mindset—having a positive outlook in challenging situations and willing to look for ways to make a situation better.

hidden curriculum—the unwritten lessons, values, and perspectives that students need to learn in school for students to become a part of the school community. These are the cultural expectations, unwritten rules, and behavioral expectations that are expected of all students. For newcomers, and especially for SLIFE, these need to be explained and taught.

hyperarousal—when someone is constantly on edge, just waiting for something to happen (especially something negative, but not exclusively).

hypervigilance—watching for something to happen, being constantly careful, or overtly sensitive to to hidden dangers from people and/or something in the environment. It can inhibit the learner academically and socially.

immigrant—a person who was born outside the United States and who has moved to this country with the intention to live here indefinitely.

infographic—a visual or other form of media to display an idea, information, or data.

L2—an abbreviation for *second language,* such as English, but used for any language learned after a person's first or native language, which is referred to as their L1.

migration narratives—stories written by or about people who are moving from one location to another.

mixed status households—family members and others living together whose members have either legal status, are naturalized or native-born citizens, and include others who arrived in the U.S. illegally and are undocumented.

mood meter—a way for someone to show quickly how they feel by pointing to an icon on a poster and/or stating a single word or phrase.

morning meetings—short introductory time for teachers and students to start a lesson, share updates, and previewing coming events.

mural—a large artwork or painting, often depicting an event or series of events.

newcomer—a student, for purposes of this book, who has been in the United States less than two years and who has developing English skills. The term does not refer to the immigration status of the child, but to the length of time in the country.

Northern Triangle—a term that refers to the three countries in Central America from which many migrants are coming: Guatemala, El Salvador, and Honduras.

pedagogical neglect—when children have not been given a fair opportunity to have a quality education for whatever reason.

perimigration—all aspects of the migration experience, from the time before departing home country through the migration journey until resettlement.

post-traumatic stress disorder (PTSD)—a reaction by the body to long-term stress that can be manifested by physical, emotional, and/or mental distress.

refugee—a person who is forced to leave his or her country and seek protection elsewhere. The United Nations High Commissioner for Refugees has the global responsibility to care for anyone who meets its criteria: someone in danger of persecution because of race, religion, nationality, political opinion or membership in a particular social group.

resilience—the capacity to and process of recovery from a single event or long-term trauma or traumatic experiences, threats, violence, and other difficulties.

restorative circles—an opportunity for people to sit and share experiences and discuss feelings with the objective to help to resolve issues and conflicts.

saludogens—factors or actions that support good health and well-being, as opposed to pathogens, which harm the body.

scattergram—a visual presentation of data, represented by dots placed above and below a baseline.

secondary traumatic stress—the body's reaction to being exposed to the stress of others, which can have similar manifestations as the stress experienced by the initial person. This type of stress can be experienced by health care professions, teachers, and in family caregivers as well.

self-actualization—the fulfillment of one's potential, according to Maslow's Hierarchy of Needs.

self-care—taking care of oneself to be better able to give quality care to others.

SIFE/SLIFE—refer to students who have experienced an interruption in their education. **SIFE** is the older of the two acronyms and stands for Students with Interrupted Formal Education. The newer term growing in popularity is **SLIFE** (Students with Limited or Interrupted Formal Education) with the *L* added to refer to the fact that some of these students have more than just interrupted schooling; it may be limited or in some cases non-existent.

social-emotional learning (SEL) standards—a list of desired actions and outcomes to be implemented in classrooms, either as stand-alone lessons or in conjunction with academic content.

testimonial therapy—an informal type of therapy that allows the victim of an event the opportunity to write or talk about the event in a therapeutic manner to release the past and move on.

toxic stress—stress that occurs a sustained period of time, similar to complex trauma or chronic stress.

transition shock—experienced by a person who has moved from one place or lifestyle to another; here referring to the culture shock that many immigrants feel over the loss of their old way of life and the adjustment to their new life.

translanguaging—the strategic use of two languages during instruction to enable emergent bilinguals to draw on their full linguistic repertoire. Translanguaging strategies help students to value their bilingual identities, cultures, and bilingualism and can serve as scaffolds for instruction and help students build academic language, academic content understanding, and metalinguistic knowledge.

trauma—the effect of experiencing an event that is beyond a person's ability to cope.

trauma-sensitive school—an educational institution that has specifically and deliberately created an atmosphere and programs that support students who have experienced trauma.

trigger—an event that reminds a person, often subconsciously, of an earlier, often negative, experience that causes a reaction (such as crying, running, or flinching).

unaccompanied (refugee) minor—a child who is without adult supervision, used in an immigration context as a person under the age of 18 who does not have an adult for protection upon coming to the U.S.

universal capacity—the ability to overcome adversity and develop resilience (according to Grotberg [1995]).

References

Adkins, M. A., Birman, D., & Sample, B. (1999). *Cultural adjustment, mental health, and ESL: The refugee experience, the role of the teacher, and ESL activities.* Denver: Spring Institute of Intercultural Learning.

Ahmad, M. K., & Harrison, J. (2007, Oct. 16). Untapped potential: Cultural sensitivity—Islamic persuasive communication in health promotion program. Paper presented at the Global Communication and Development Conference, Shanghai, China.

Alaska Department of Education and Early Development. (2019). *Transforming schools: A framework for trauma-engaged practice in Alaska.* Juneau: Author.

Alvarez, K., & Alegria, M. (2016, June). *Understanding and addressing the needs of unaccompanied immigrant minors: Depression, conduct problems, and PTSD in immigrant minors.* http://www.apa.org/pi/families/resources/newsletter/2016/06/immigrant-minors.aspx

Altherr Flores, J. A., Farrelly, R., Montero, K., & Johnson, R. (2018, Mar. 28). Panel: Refugee-background students with trauma: Research, pedagogy, and community resources. Paper presented at International TESOL Convention, Chicago, IL.

American Immigration Council. (2020, June 11). *Asylum in the United States: A fact sheet.* Washington, DC: Author.

Antonovsky, A. (1996). The salutogenic model as a theory to guide health promotion. *Health Promotion International, 11*(1), 11–18.

ASCD. (2007). *The learning compact redefined: A call to action.* Alexandria, VA: Author.

ASCD. (2014). *Whole school, whole community, whole child: A collaborative approach to learning and health.* Alexandria, VA: Author.

ASCD. (2020). *The learning compact renewed: The whole child for the whole world.* Alexandria, VA: Author.

Asgedom, M. (2016). *Powerful educator: How to inspire student growth.* Chicago: Mawi Learning.

Aspen Institute. (2018, Jan. 23). *How learning happens: Supporting students' social, emotional, and academic development.* https://assets.aspeninstitute.org/content/uploads/2018/01/2017_Aspen_InterimReport_Update2.pdf

Atkins, M., Frazier, S. L., Birman, D., Adil, J. A., Jackson, M., Graczyk, P. A., Talbott, E., Farmer, A. D., Bell, C. C., & McKay, M. M. (2006). School-based mental health services for children living in high poverty urban communities. *Administration and Policy in Mental Health and Mental Health Services Research, 33*(2), 146–163.

Barth, R. S. (2002). The culture builder. *Educational Leadership, 59*(8), 6.

Berdik, C. (2019). *Fighting teacher stress.* New York: The Hechinger Report.

Berger, E., & Rojas-Cortez, M. (2016). *Parents as partners in education: Families and schools working together.* New York: Pearson.

Berman, S. Chaffee, S., & Sarmiento, J. (2018, Mar. 2). *The practice base for how we learn: Supporting students' social, emotional, and academic development.* Washington, DC: Aspen Institute.

Birman, D. (2002). *Mental health of refugee children: A guide for the ESL teacher.* Denver: Spring Institute of Intercultural Learning.

Birman, D., Weinstein, T., Chan, W. Y., & Beehler, S. (2007). Immigrant youth in U.S. schools: Opportunities for prevention. *The Prevention Researcher, 14*(4), 14–17.

Blaustein, M. (2013). Childhood trauma and a framework for intervention. In E. Rossen & R. Hull (Eds.), *Supporting and educating traumatized students: A guide for school-based professionals* (pp. 3–22). New York: Oxford University Press.

Bloom, S. (2014, Oct. 23). *Unaccompanied minors and trauma: What does it look like and what can we do?* New York: New York City Department of Education. http://www.cdfny.org/research-library/publications/2014/unaccompanied-minors-and.pdf

Bonanno, G. A. (2004). Loss, trauma, and human resilience: Have we underestimated the human capacity to thrive after extremely aversive events? *American Psychologist, 59*(1), 20–28.

Borba, M. (2018). Nine competencies for teaching empathy. *Educational Leadership, 76*(2), 22–28.

Brackett, M. (2018). The emotional intelligence we owe our students and teachers. *Educational Leadership, 76*(2), 12–18.

Brown, J. (2008). *Educating the whole child.* Alexandria, VA: ASCD.

Carey, R. J., & Kim, J. S. (2010). Tapping the potential of refugee youth. In G. Sonnert & G. Holton (Eds.), *Helping young refugee and immigrants succeed: Public policy, aid, and education* (pp. 191–208). New York: Palgrave Macmillan.

Cheatham, A. (2020). *U.S. detention of child migrants.* New York: Council on Foreign Relations.

Collaborative for Academic, Social, and Emotional Learning. (2012). *2013 CASEL guide: Effective social and emotional learning programs—preschool and elementary school edition.* Chicago: Author.

Collaborative for Academic, Social and Emotional Learning. (2015). *2015 CASEL guide: Effective social and emotional learning programs—middle and high school edition.* Chicago: Author.

Collaborative for Academic, Social and Emotional Learning. (2017). *Personal assessment and reflection—SEL competencies for school leaders, staff and adults.* Chicago: Author.

Craig, S. (2017). *Trauma-sensitive schools for the adolescent years: Promoting resiliency and healing, grades 6-12.* New York: Teachers College Press.

Cummins, J., Bismilla, V., Chow, P., Cohen, S., Giampapa, F., Leoni, L., Sandhu, P., & Sastri, P. (2005). Affirming identity in multicultural classrooms. *Educational Leadership, 63*(1), 38–43.

Custodio, B., & O'Loughlin, J.B. (2017). *Students with interrupted formal education: Bridging where they are and what they need.* Thousand Oaks, CA: Corwin Press.

de Oliveira, L., & Wachter Morris, C. A. (2015). *Preparing school counselors for English language learners.* Alexandria, VA: TESOL.

DeCapua, A., Marshall, H., & Tang, F. L. (2020). *Meeting the needs of SLIFE: A guide for educators* (2nd ed.). Ann Arbor: University of Michigan Press.

DeCapua, A., Smathers, W., & Tang, F. L. (2009). *Meeting the needs of students with limited or interrupted schooling.* Ann Arbor: University of Michigan Press.

Digby, S. (2019). *Supporting Latino students with interrupted formal education: A guide for teachers.* (Resource Guide Volume 5.) New York: Institute of Latin American Studies, Columbia University.

Duval, S. (2018). Antiracist practices: strengthening students' sense of self to promote hope and confidence for student success. In S. Wong, E. S. Gosnell, A. M. F. Luu, & L. Dodson (Eds.), *Teachers as allies: Transformative practices for teaching DREAMers and undocumented students* (pp. 45–58). New York: Teachers College Press.

Dweck, C. (2015). Carol Dweck revisits "growth mindset." *Education Week, 35*(5), 20–24.

El Yaafouri, L. (2018, Aug. 31). Strategies for easing transition shock. *Edutopia.* https://www.edutopia.org/article/strategies-easing-transition-shock

Felitti, V. J., Anda, R. F., Nordenberg, D., Williamson, D. F., Spitz, A. M., Edwards, V., Koss, M. P., & Marks, J. S. (1998). Relationship of childhood abuse and household dysfunction to many of the leading causes of death in adults: The Adverse Childhood Experiences (ACE) Study. *American Journal of Preventive Medicine, 14*(4), 245–258.

Flaitz, J. (2006). *Understanding your refugee and immigrant students: An educational, cultural, and linguistic guide.* Ann Arbor: University of Michigan Press.

Fleming, N. (2019, June 14). Why diverse classroom libraries matter. *Edutopia.* www.edutopia.org/article/why-diverse-classrooms-libraries-matter.

Fletcher, J. (2018, June 19). Paper tweets build SEL skills. *Edutopia.* www.edutopia.org/article/paper-tweets-build-sel-skills

Foster, R. P. (2001). When immigration is trauma: Guidelines for the individual and family clinician. *American Journal of Orthopsychiatry, 71*(2), 153–170.

Freeman, D., Freeman, Y., & Soto, M. (2016). Translanguaging success into practice. *Language Magazine, 16*(4), 18–21.

García, O., & Wei, L. (2014). *Translanguaging: Language, bilingualism and education.* New York: Palgrave Macmillan.

Granello, P. (2019, Feb. 18). *The importance of stress management and relaxation for emotional wellness.* Workshop given at The Ohio State University, Columbus.

Green, A., & Kelley, C. (2016, Nov. 16). *Trauma-informed care of immigrant and refugee children.* https://www.futureswithoutviolence.org/wp-content/uploads/WebinarTrauma-Informed-Care-Immigrant-and-Refugee.pdf

Grotberg. E. (1995). *A guide to promoting resilience in children: Strengthening the human spirit. Early childhood development: Practice and reflections.* (Number 8.) The Netherlands: Bernard van Leer Foundation. https://bibalex.org/baifa/Attachment/Documents/115519.pdf

Hamman, L., Beck, E., & Donaldson, A. (2018). A pedagogy of translanguaging. *Language Magazine.* https://www.languagemagazine.com/2018/09/10/a-pedagogy-of-translanguaging/

Hamre, B., & Pianta, R. (2007). Learning opportunities in preschool and early elementary classrooms. In R. Pianta, M. Cox, & K. Snow (Eds.), *School readiness and the transition to kindergarten in the era of accountability* (pp. 49–83). Baltimore: Brookes Publishing.

Herman, K., Hickmon-Rosa, J., & Reinke, W. (2018, April). Empirically derived profiles of teacher stress, burnout, self-efficacy, and coping and associated student outcomes. *Journal of Positive Behavior Interventions, 20*(2), 90–100.

Hertel, R., & Johnson, M. (2013). How the traumatic experiences of students manifest in school settings. In E. Rossen & R. Hull (Eds), *Supporting and educating traumatized students: A guide for school-based professionals* (pp. 23–36). New York: Oxford University Press.

Interdisciplinary Association for Population Health Science. (2019, Nov. 18). *Borders of belonging: Mixed status families and the impact of family separation on population health*. Clearfield, UT: Author.

Jerald, C. (2006). *School culture: "The hidden curriculum."* Washington, DC: The Center for Comprehensive School Reform and Improvement.

Johnson, S., Cooper, C., Cartwright, S., Donald, I., Taylor, P., & Millet, C. (2005). The experience of work-related stress across occupations. *Journal of Managerial Psychology, 20*(2), 178–187. https://www.emeraldinsight.com/doi/abs/10.1108/02683940510579803

Johnson, T. (2018, Mar. 14). How aggressive immigration enforcement hurts America's schools. *Immigration Impact*. http://immigrationimpact.com/2018/03/14/immigration-enforcement-hurts-schools/

Kamarck, E., & Stenglein, C. (2019). *How many undocumented immigrants are in the United States and who are they?* Washington, DC: Brookings Institution.

Kennedy, E. (2014). *No childhood here: Why Central American children are fleeing their homes*. Washington, DC: American Immigration Council.

Konnikova, M. (2016, Feb. 11). How people learn to become resilient. *The New Yorker*. https://www.newyorker.com/science/maria-konnikova/the-secret-formula-for-resilience

Lee, H., Griffin, R.M., Keels, M. (2018). *Maintaining educator well-being*. Chicago: Trauma Responsive Educational Practices Project.

Lee, V. J., Hoekje, B., & Levine, B. (2018). Introducing technology to immigrant families to support early literary development and two-generation learning. *Language Arts: A National Council of Teachers of English Journal, 95*(3), 133–148.

Loukas, A. (2007). What is school climate? High quality school climate is advantageous for all students and may be particularly beneficial for at-risk students. *Leadership Compass, 5*(1), 1–3.

Lukes, M. (2015). *Latino immigrant youth and interrupted schooling: Dropouts, dreamers, and alternative pathways to college.* Bristol, England: Multilingual Matters.

Mapp, K., & Kuttner, P. (2013). *Partners in education: A dual capacity-building framework for family-school partnerships.* Washington, DC: SEDL and the U.S. Department of Education.

Mashburn, A., & Pianta, R. (2006). Social development and school readiness. *Early Education and Development, 17*(1), 151–176.

Maslow, A.H. (1943). A theory of human motivation. *Psychological Review, 50*(4), 370–396.

Masten, A., Best, K., & Garmezy, N. (1990). Resilience and development: Contributions from the study of children who overcome adversity. *Development and Psychopathology, 2(*4), 425–444.

McElhiney, A. (n.d.). Resilience: A necessary ingredient in overcoming cancer. *The Clearity Foundation.* [blog]. https://www.clearityfoundation.org/resilience-a-necessary-ingredient-in-overcoming-cancer/

McKibben, S. (2018). Grit and the greater good: A conversation with Angela Duckworth. *Educational Leadership, 76*(2), 40–45.

Merz, S. (2017/2018). Who in your class needs help? *Educational Leadership, 75*(4), 12–17.

Miller, C. (n.d.) *Anxiety and disruptive behavior in children.* New York: Child Mind Institute. https://childmind.org/article/how-anxiety-leads-to)-disruptive-behavior/

Minero, E. (2017, Oct. 4). When students are traumatized, teachers are too. *Edutopia.* www.edutopia.org/article/when-students-are-traumatized-teachers-are-too

Minero, E. (2019, Feb. 5). 10 powerful community building ideas. *Edutopia.* www.edutopia.org/article/10-powerful-community-building-ideas

Mirano, H. E. (2003, May 1). The art of resilience. *Psychology Today.* Retrieved from https://www.psychologytoday.com/us/articles/200305/the-art-resilience

Morland, L., Birman, D., Dunn, B. L., Adkins, M.A, & Gardner, L. (2013). Immigrant students. In E. Rossen & R. Hull (Eds.), *Supporting and educating traumatized students: A guide for school-based professionals* (pp. 51–72). New York: Oxford University Press.

Morland, L., & Birman, D. (2020). Immigrant students. In E. Rossen & R. Hull (Eds.), *Supporting and educating traumatized students* (2nd ed., pp. 101–124). New York: Oxford University Press.

National Association of School Psychologists. (2015). *Supporting refugee children and youth: Tips for educators.* Bethesda, MD: Author.

National Center on Safe Supportive Learning Environments. (n.d.). *Secondary traumatic stress and self-care packet.* Washington, DC: American Institutes for Research.

National Child Traumatic Stress Network. (2007). *Culture and trauma brief: Preliminary adaptations for working with traumatized Latino/Hispanic children and their families,* 2(3). Los Angeles: Author. http://www.nctsn.org/nctsn_assets/pdfs/culture_and_trauma_brief_v2n3_LatinoHispanicChildren.pdf

National Child Traumatic Stress Network. (2008). *Child trauma toolkit for educators.* Los Angeles: Author.

National Child Traumatic Stress Network. (2011). *Secondary traumatic stress: A fact sheet for child serving professionals.* Los Angeles: Author. https://www.nctsn.org/resources/secondary-traumatic-stress-fact-sheet-child-serving-professionals

Palmer, P. (2019). *The teacher self-care manual: Simple strategies for stressed teachers.* Branford, CT: Alphabet Publishing.

Peralta, C. (2019). Why are we still blaming the families in 2019? *The Reading Teacher, 72*(5), 670–673.

Peterson, C., Ruch, W., Beermann, U., Park, N., & Seligman, M. E. P. (2007). Strengths of character, orientations to happiness, and life satisfaction, *The Journal of Positive Psychology, 2*(3), 149–156. doi: 10.1080/17439760701228938

Ramirez, A. (2017, Nov. 14). Latino childhood development research: Childhood trauma. The state of Latino early childhood development: A research review. *Salud America*! https://salud-america.org/wp-content/uploads/2017/11/Early-Child-Dev-Res-Review.pdf

Ravitz, A. (2019). *How to foster resilience in kids.* New York: Child Mind Institute. https://childmind.org/article/foster-resilience-kids/

Ristuccia, J. M. (2013). Creating safe and supportive schools for students impacted by traumatic experience. In E. Rossen & R. Hull (Eds.), *Supporting and educating traumatized students: A guide for school-based professionals* (pp. 251–264). New York: Oxford University Press.

Rossen, E., & Hull, R. (Eds.). (2013). *Supporting and educating traumatized students: A guide for school-based professionals.* New York: Oxford University Press.

Schmelzer, G. L. (2018). *Journey through trauma: A trail guide to the 5-phase cycle of healing repeated trauma.* New York: Penguin Random House.

Schwartz, R. (2018, June 28). Why are so many children coming to the U.S. from Central America anyway? *Washington Post.*

Scullen, J. (2019). Keys to a culture of literacy. *Literacy Today, 37*(1), 8–9.

Sehgal, P. (2015, Dec. 6). *The profound emptiness of resilience.* https://www.nytimes.com/2015/12/06/magazine/the-profound-emptiness-of-resilience.html.

Short, D. J. (2019, July 17). Our beloved community. Keynote address at SIOP National Conference, Portland, OR.

Souers, K. (December 2017/ January 2018). Responding with care to students facing trauma. *Educational Leadership,* 32–36.

Souers, K. (with Hall, P.) (2016). *Fostering resilient learners: Strategies for creating a trauma-sensitive classroom.* Alexandria, VA: ASCD.

Starr, D. (2011*). From bombs to books.* Toronto: James Lorimer and Company, Ltd.

Stewart, M. A. (2015). My journey of hope and peace. *Journal of Adolescent and Adult Literacy, 59*(2), 149–159.

Stewart, W. (2017) *Mindful kids: 50 mindfulness activities for kindness, focus, and calm.* Cambridge, MA: Barefoot Books.

Stoeber, J., & Rennert, D. (2008). Perfectionism in school teachers: Relations with stress appriaisals, coping styles, and burnout. *Anxiety, Stress & Coping, 21(1*), 37–53. doi: 10.1080/1061580070174261.

TESOL International Association. (2018). *The 6 principles for exemplary teaching of English learners: Grades K–12.* Alexandria, VA: Author.

Thomas, L. (2018, May 23). Morning meetings in middle and high school. *Edutopia.* www.edutopia.org/article/morning-meetings-middle-and-high-school

Thorp, E. (2018). Teachers as allies and advocates for students living in fear of raids, detention, and deportation. In S. Wong, E.S. Gosnell, A. M. F. Luu, & L. Dodson (Eds.), *Teachers as allies: Transformative practices for teaching DREAMers and undocumented students* (pp. 35–42). New York: Teachers College Press.

Transactional Records Access Clearinghouse (TRAC) Immigration. (2020, June 8). *Record number of asylum cases in the United States.* Syracuse, NY: Syracuse University.

United Nations High Commissioner for Refugees. (2014). *Children on the run: Unaccompanied children leaving Central America and Mexico and the need for international protection.* Washington, DC: Author.

United Nations High Commissioner for Refugees. (2019). *Stepping up: Refugee education in crisis.* Washington, DC: Author.

U.S. Department of Education. (2016). *Newcomer tool kit.* https://www2.ed.gov/about/offices/list/oela/newcomers-toolkit/ncomertoolkit.pdf

Van der Veer, G. (1998). *Counselling and therapy with refugees and victims of trauma: Psychological problems of victims of war, torture and repression.* New York: John Wiley and Sons.

Werner, E. E., & Smith, R. S. (2001). *Journeys from childhood to midlife: Risk, resilience, and recovery.* Ithaca, NY: Cornell University Press.

Wilkins, G. M. (2019, April 1). *Testimonial Therapy.* Catholic Charities of Dayton. Paper presented at the Cultural Aspects of Refugee Mental Health Conference, Dayton, OH.

Wink, J. (2018). *The power of story.* Santa Barbara, CA: Libraries Unlimited.

Wolpow, R., Johnson, M., Hertel, R., & Kincaid, S. (2009). *The heart of learning and teaching: Compassion, resilience, and academic success.* Tacoma: Washington State Office of the Superintendent of Public Instruction.

World Health Organization. (2015). *Adverse childhood experiences-International questionnaire.* http://www.who.int/violence_injury_prevention/violence/activities/adverse_childhood_experiences/en/

Zacarian, D., Alvarez-Ortiz, L., & Haynes, J. (2017). *Teaching to strengths: Supporting students living with trauma, violence, and chronic stress.* Alexandria, VA: ASCD.

Zehr, H. (1990). "A restorative lens" in changing lenses: A new focus for crime and justice. In T. Gavrielides (Ed.), *Restorative justice: Ideals and realities* (pp. 177–214). Waterloo, Ontario: Herald Press.

Index

Printed and bound by CPI Group (UK) Ltd, Croydon, CR0 4YY

13/04/2025

14656541-0003